JAMESTOWN EDU

MW01153235

Timed Readings Plus
in Social Studies

BOOK 8

**25 Two-Part Lessons with Questions for
Building Reading Speed and Comprehension**

 McGraw Hill **Glencoe**

New York, New York   Columbus, Ohio   Chicago, Illinois   Peoria, Illinois   Woodland Hills, California

JAMESTOWN EDUCATION

Glencoe

The *McGraw·Hill* Companies

ISBN: 0-07-845806-4

Send all queries to:
Glencoe/McGraw-Hill
8787 Orion Place
Columbus, OH 43240-4027

6 7 8 9 10 DOH 15 14

CONTENTS

To the Student

    Reading Faster and Better   2

    Mastering Reading Comprehension   3

    Working Through a Lesson   7

    Plotting Your Progress   8

To the Teacher

    About the Series   9

    Timed Reading and Comprehension   10

    Speed Versus Comprehension   10

    Getting Started   10

    Timing the Reading   11

    Teaching a Lesson   11

    Monitoring Progress   12

    Diagnosis and Evaluation   12

Lessons   13–112

Answer Key   114–115

Graphs   116–118

To the Student

You probably talk at an average rate of about 150 words a minute. If you are a reader of average ability, you read at a rate of about 250 words a minute. So your reading speed is nearly twice as fast as your speaking or listening speed. This example shows that reading is one of the fastest ways to get information.

The purpose of this book is to help you increase your reading rate and understand what you read. The 25 lessons in this book will also give you practice in reading social studies articles and in preparing for tests in which you must read and understand nonfiction passages within a certain time limit.

Reading Faster and Better

Following are some strategies that you can use to read the articles in each lesson.

Previewing

Previewing before you read is a very important step. This helps you to get an idea of what a selection is about and to recall any previous knowledge you have about the subject. Here are the steps to follow when previewing.

Read the title. Titles are designed not only to announce the subject but also to make the reader think. Ask yourself questions such as What can I learn from the title? What thoughts does it bring to mind?

What do I already know about this subject?

Read the first sentence. If they are short, read the first two sentences. The opening sentence is the writer's opportunity to get your attention. Some writers announce what they hope to tell you in the selection. Some writers state their purpose for writing; others just try to get your attention.

Read the last sentence. If it is short, read the final two sentences. The closing sentence is the writer's last chance to get ideas across to you. Some writers repeat the main idea once more. Some writers draw a conclusion—this is what they have been leading up to. Other writers summarize their thoughts; they tie all the facts together.

Skim the entire selection. Glance through the selection quickly to see what other information you can pick up. Look for anything that will help you read fluently and with under-standing. Are there names, dates, or numbers? If so, you may have to read more slowly.

Reading for Meaning

Here are some ways to make sure you are making sense of what you read.

Build your concentration. You cannot understand what you read if you are not concentrating. When you discover that your thoughts are straying, correct the situation right away. Avoid distractions and distracting situations. Keep in mind the information you learned from previewing. This will help focus your attention on the selection.

Read in thought groups. Try to see meaningful combinations of words—phrases, clauses, or sentences. If you look at only one word at a time (called word-by-word reading), both your comprehension and your reading speed suffer.

Ask yourself questions. To sustain the pace you have set for yourself and to maintain a high level of concentration and comprehension, ask yourself questions such as What does this mean? or How can I use this information? as you read.

Finding the Main Ideas

The paragraph is the basic unit of meaning. If you can quickly discover and understand the main idea of each paragraph, you will build your comprehension of the selection.

Find the topic sentence. The topic sentence, which contains the main idea, often is the first sentence of a paragraph. It is followed by sentences that support, develop, or explain the main idea. Sometimes a topic sentence comes at the end of a paragraph. When it does, the supporting details come first, building the base for the topic sentence. Some paragraphs do not have a topic sentence; all of the sentences combine to create a meaningful idea.

Understand paragraph structure. Every well-written paragraph has a purpose. The purpose may be to inform, define, explain, or illustrate. The purpose should always relate to the main idea and expand on it. As you read each paragraph, see how the body of the paragraph tells you more about the main idea.

Relate ideas as you read. As you read the selection, notice how the writer puts together ideas. As you discover the relationship between the ideas, the main ideas come through quickly and clearly.

Mastering Reading Comprehension

Reading fast is not useful if you don't remember or understand what you read. The two exercises in Part A provide a check on how well you have understood the article.

Recalling Facts

These multiple-choice questions provide a quick check to see how well you recall important information from the article. As you learn to apply the reading strategies described earlier, you should be able to answer these questions more successfully.

Understanding Ideas

These questions require you to think about the main ideas in the article. Some main ideas are stated in the article; others are not. To answer some of the questions, you need to draw conclusions about what you read.

The five exercises in Part B require multiple answers. These exercises provide practice in applying comprehension and critical thinking skills that you can use in all your reading.

Recognizing Words in Context

Always check to see whether the words around an unfamiliar word—its context—can give you a clue to the word's meaning. A word generally appears in a context related to its meaning.

Suppose, for example, that you are unsure of the meaning of the word *expired* in the following passage:

> Vera wanted to check out a book, but her library card had expired. She had to borrow my card, because she didn't have time to renew hers.

You could begin to figure out the meaning of *expired* by asking yourself a question such as, What could have happened to Vera's library card that would make her need to borrow someone else's card? You might realize that if Vera had to renew her card, its usefulness must have come to an end or run out. This would lead you to conclude that the word *expired* must mean "to come to an end" or "to run out." You would be right. The context suggested the meaning.

Context can also affect the meaning of a word you already know. The word *key*, for instance, has many meanings. There are musical keys, door keys, and keys to solving a mystery. The context in which the word *key* occurs will tell you which meaning is correct.

Sometimes a word is explained by the words that immediately follow it. The subject of a sentence and your knowledge about that subject might also help you determine the meaning of an unknown word. Try to decide the meaning of the word *revive* in the following sentence:

> Sunshine and water will revive those drooping plants.

The compound subject is *sunshine* and *water*. You know that plants need light and water to survive and that drooping plants are not healthy. You can figure out that *revive* means "to bring back to health."

Distinguishing Fact from Opinion

Every day you are called upon to sort out fact and opinion. Because much of what you read and hear contains both facts and opinions, you need to be able to tell the two apart.

Facts are statements that can be proved. The proof must be objective and verifiable. You must be able to check for yourself to confirm a fact.

Look at the following facts. Notice that they can be checked for accuracy and confirmed. Suggested sources for verification appear in parentheses.

- Abraham Lincoln was the 16th president of the United States. (Consult biographies, social studies books, encyclopedias, and similar sources.)

- Earth revolves around the Sun. (Research in encyclopedias or astronomy books; ask knowledgeable people.)

- Dogs walk on four legs. (See for yourself.)

Opinions are statements that cannot be proved. There is no objective evidence you can consult to check the truthfulness of an opinion. Unlike facts, opinions express personal beliefs or judgments. Opinions reveal how someone feels about a subject, not the facts about that subject. You might agree or disagree with someone's opinion, but you cannot prove it right or wrong.

Look at the following opinions. The reasons these statements are classified as opinions appear in parentheses.

- Abraham Lincoln was born to be a president. (You cannot prove this by referring to birth records. There is no evidence to support this belief.)

- Earth is the only planet in our solar system where intelligent life exists. (There is no proof of this. It may be proved true some day, but for now it is just an educated guess—not a fact.)

- The dog is a human's best friend. (This is not a fact; your best friend might not be a dog.)

As you read, be aware that facts and opinions are often mixed together. Both are useful to you as a reader. But to evaluate what you read and to read intelligently, you need to know the difference between the two.

Keeping Events in Order

Sequence, or chronological order, is the order of events in a story or article or the order of steps in a process. Paying attention to the sequence of events or steps will help you follow what is happening, predict what might happen next, and make sense of a passage.

To make the sequence as clear as possible, writers often use signal words to help the reader get a more exact idea of when things happen. Following is a list of frequently used signal words and phrases:

until	first
next	then
before	after
finally	later
when	while
during	now
at the end	by the time
as soon as	in the beginning

Signal words and phrases are also useful when a writer chooses to relate details or events out of sequence. You need to pay careful attention to determine the correct chronological order.

Making Correct Inferences

Much of what you read *suggests* more than it *says*. Writers often do not state ideas directly in a text. They can't. Think of the time and space it would take to state every idea. And think of how boring that would be! Instead, writers leave it to you, the reader, to fill in the information they leave out—to make inferences. You do this by combining clues in the story or article with knowledge from your own experience.

You make many inferences every day. Suppose, for example, that you are visiting a friend's house for the first time. You see a bag of kitty litter. You infer (make an inference) that the family has a cat. Another day you overhear a conversation. You catch the names of two actors and the words *scene, dialogue,* and *directing.* You infer that the people are discussing a movie or play.

In these situations and others like them, you infer unstated information from what you observe or read. Readers must make inferences in order to understand text.

Be careful about the inferences you make. One set of facts may suggest several inferences. Some of these inferences could be faulty. A correct inference must be supported by evidence.

Remember that bag of kitty litter that caused you to infer that your friend has a cat? That could be a faulty inference. Perhaps your friend's family uses the kitty litter on their icy sidewalks to create traction. To be sure your inference is correct, you need more evidence.

Understanding Main Ideas

The main idea is the most important idea in a paragraph or passage—the idea that provides purpose and direction. The rest of the selection explains, develops, or supports the main idea. Without a main idea, there would be only a collection of unconnected thoughts.

In the following paragraph, the main idea is printed in italics. As you read, observe how the other sentences develop or explain the main idea.

Typhoon Chris hit with full fury today on the central coast of Japan. Heavy rain from the storm flooded the area. High waves carried many homes into the sea. People now fear that the heavy rains will cause mudslides in the central part of the country. The number of people killed by the storm may climb past the 200 mark by Saturday.

In this paragraph, the main-idea statement appears first. It is followed by sentences that explain, support, or give details. Sometimes the main idea appears at the end of a paragraph. Writers often put the main idea at the end of a paragraph when their purpose is to persuade or convince. Readers may be more open to a new idea if the reasons for it are presented first.

As you read the following paragraph, think about the overall impact of the supporting ideas. Their purpose is to convince the reader that the main idea in the last sentence should be accepted.

Last week there was a head-on collision at Huntington and Canton streets. Just a month ago a pedestrian was struck there. Fortunately, she was only slightly injured. In the past year, there have been more accidents there than at any other corner in the city. In fact, nearly 10 percent of all accidents in the city occur at the corner. This intersection is very dangerous, and a traffic signal should be installed there before a life is lost.

The details in the paragraph progress from least important to most important. They achieve their full effect in the main idea statement at the end.

In many cases, the main idea is not expressed in a single sentence. The reader is called upon to interpret all of the ideas expressed in the paragraph and to decide upon a main idea. Read the following paragraph.

> The American author Jack London was once a pupil at the Cole Grammar School in Oakland, California. Each morning the class sang a song. When the teacher noticed that Jack wouldn't sing, she sent him to the principal. He returned to class with a note. The note said that Jack could be excused from singing with the class if he would write an essay every morning.

In this paragraph, the reader has to interpret the individual ideas and to decide on a main idea. This main idea seems reasonable: Jack London's career as a writer began with a punishment in grammar school.

Understanding the concept of the main idea and knowing how to find it is important. Transferring that understanding to your reading and study is also important.

Working Through a Lesson

Part A

1. **Preview the article.** Locate the timed selection in Part A of the lesson that you are going to read. Wait for your teacher's signal to preview. You will have 20 seconds for previewing. Follow the previewing steps described on page 2.

2. **Read the article.** When your teacher gives you the signal, begin reading. Read carefully so that you will be able to answer questions about what you have read. When you finish reading, look at the board and note your reading time. Write this time at the bottom of the page on the line labeled Reading Time.

3. **Complete the exercises.** Answer the 10 questions that follow the article. There are 5 fact questions and 5 idea questions. Choose the best answer to each question and put an X in that box.

4. **Correct your work.** Use the Answer Key at the back of the book to check your answers. Circle any wrong answer and put an X in the box you should have marked. Record the number of correct answers on the appropriate line at the end of the lesson.

Part B

1. **Preview and read the passage.** Use the same techniques you

used to read Part A. Think about what you are reading.

2. **Complete the exercises.** Instructions are given for answering each category of question. There are 15 responses for you to record.

3. **Correct your work.** Use the Answer Key at the back of the book. Circle any wrong answer and write the correct letter or number next to it. Record the number of correct answers on the appropriate line at the end of the lesson.

Plotting Your Progress

1. **Find your reading rate.** Turn to the Reading Rate graph on page 116. Put an X at the point where the vertical line that represents the lesson intersects your reading time, shown along the left-hand side. The right-hand side of the graph will reveal your words-per-minute reading speed.

2. **Find your comprehension score.** Add your scores for Part A and Part B to determine your total number of correct answers. Turn to the Comprehension Score Graph on page 117. Put an X at the point where the vertical line that represents your lesson intersects your total correct answers, shown along the left-hand side. The right-hand side of the graph will show the percentage of questions you answered correctly.

3. **Complete the Comprehension Skills Profile.** Turn to page 118. Record your incorrect answers for the Part B exercises. The five Part B skills are listed along the bottom. There are five columns of boxes, one column for each question. For every incorrect answer, put an X in a box for that skill.

To get the most benefit from these lessons, you need to take charge of your own progress in improving your reading speed and comprehension. Studying these graphs will help you to see whether your reading rate is increasing and to determine what skills you need to work on. Your teacher will also review the graphs to check your progress.

TO THE TEACHER

About the Series

Timed Readings Plus in Social Studies includes 10 books at reading levels 4–13, with one book at each level. Book One contains material at a fourth-grade reading level; Book Two at a fifth-grade level, and so on. The readability level is determined by the Fry Readability Scale and is not to be confused with grade or age level of the student. The books are designed for use with students at middle school level and above.

The purposes of the series are as follows:

- to provide systematic, structured reading practice that helps students improve their reading rate and comprehension skills

- to give students practice in reading and understanding informational articles in the content area of social studies

- to give students experience in reading various text types—informational, expository, narrative, and prescriptive

- to prepare students for taking standardized tests that include timed reading passages in various content areas

- to provide materials with a wide range of reading levels so that students can continue to practice and improve their reading rate and comprehension skills

Because the books are designed for use with students at designated reading levels rather than in a particular grade, the social studies topics in this series are not correlated to any grade-level curriculum. Most standardized tests require students to read and comprehend social studies passages. This series provides an opportunity for students to become familiar with the particular requirements of reading social studies. For example, the vocabulary in a social studies article is important. Students need to know certain words in order to understand the concepts and the information.

Each book in the series contains 25 two-part lessons. Part A focuses on improving reading rate. This section of the lesson consists of a 400-word timed informational article on a social studies topic followed by two multiple-choice exercises. Recalling Facts includes five fact questions; Understanding Ideas includes five critical thinking questions.

Part B concentrates on building mastery in critical areas of comprehension. This section consists of a nontimed passage—the "plus" passage—followed by five exercises that address five major comprehension skills. The passage varies in length; its subject matter relates to the content of the timed selection.

Timed Reading and Comprehension

Timed reading is the best-known method of improving reading speed. There is no point in someone's reading at an accelerated speed if the person does not understand what she or he is reading. Nothing is more important than comprehension in reading. The main purpose of reading is to gain knowledge and insight, to understand the information that the writer and the text are communicating.

Few students will be able to read a passage once and answer all of the questions correctly. A score of 70 or 80 percent correct is normal. If the student gets 90 or 100 percent correct, he or she is either reading too slowly or the material is at too low a reading level. A comprehension or critical thinking score of less than 70 percent indicates a need for improvement.

One method of improving comprehension and critical thinking skills is for the student to go back and study each incorrect answer. First, the student should reread the question carefully. It is surprising how many students get the wrong answer simply because they have not read the question carefully. Then the student should look back in the passage to find the place where the question is answered, reread that part of the passage, and think about how to arrive at the correct answer. It is important to be able to recognize a correct answer when it

is embedded in the text. Teacher guidance or class discussion will help the student find an answer.

Speed Versus Comprehension

It is not unusual for comprehension scores to decline as reading rate increases during the early weeks of timed readings. If this happens, students should attempt to level off their speed—but not lower it—and concentrate more on comprehension. Usually, if students maintain the higher speed and concentrate on comprehension, scores will gradually improve and within a week or two be back up to normal levels of 70 to 80 percent.

It is important to achieve a proper balance between speed and comprehension. An inefficient reader typically reads everything at one speed, usually slowly. Some poor readers, however, read rapidly but without satisfactory comprehension. It is important to achieve a balance between speed and comprehension. The practice that this series provides enables students to increase their reading speed while maintaining normal levels of comprehension.

Getting Started

As a rule, the passages in a book designed to improve reading speed should be relatively easy. The student should not have much difficulty with the vocabulary or the subject matter. Don't worry about the passages being too easy; students should see how quickly and efficiently they can read a passage.

Begin by assigning students to a level. A student should start with a book that is one level below his or her current reading level. If a student's reading level is not known, a suitable starting point would be one or two levels below the student's present grade in school.

Introduce students to the contents and format of the book they are using. Examine the book to see how it is organized. Talk about the parts of each lesson. Discuss the purpose of timed reading and the use of the progress graphs at the back of the book.

Timing the Reading

One suggestion for timing the reading is to have all students begin reading the selection at the same time. After one minute, write on the board the time that has elapsed and begin updating it at 10-second intervals (1:00, 1:10, 1:20, etc.). Another option is to have individual students time themselves with a stopwatch.

Teaching a Lesson

Part A

1. Give students the signal to begin previewing the lesson. Allow 20 seconds, then discuss special terms or vocabulary that students found.

2. Use one of the methods described above to time students as they read the passage. (Include the 20-second preview time as part of the first minute.) Tell students to write down the last time shown on the board or the stopwatch when they finish reading. Have them record the time in the designated space after the passage.

3. Next, have students complete the exercises in Part A. Work with them to check their answers, using the Answer Key that begins on page 114. Have them circle incorrect answers, mark the correct answers, and then record the numbers of correct answers for Part A on the appropriate line at the end of the lesson. Correct responses to eight or more questions indicate satisfactory comprehension and recall.

Part B

1. Have students read the Part B passage and complete the exercises that follow it. Directions are provided with each exercise. Correct responses require deliberation and discrimination.

2. Work with students to check their answers. Then discuss the answers with them and have them record the number of correct answers for Part B at the end of the lesson.

Have students study the correct answers to the questions they answered incorrectly. It is important that they understand why a particular answer is correct or incorrect.

Have them reread relevant parts of a passage to clarify an answer. An effective cooperative activity is to have students work in pairs to discuss their answers, explain why they chose the answers they did, and try to resolve differences.

Monitoring Progress

Have students find their total correct answers for the lesson and record their reading time and scores on the graphs on pages 116 and 117. Then have them complete the Comprehension Skills Profile on page 118. For each incorrect response to a question in Part B, students should mark an X in the box above each question type.

The legend on the Reading Rate graph automatically converts reading times to words-per-minute rates. The Comprehension Score graph automatically converts the raw scores to percentages.

These graphs provide a visual record of a student's progress. This record gives the student and you an opportunity to evaluate the student's progress and to determine the types of exercises and skills he or she needs to concentrate on.

Diagnosis and Evaluation

The following are typical reading rates.

Slow Reader—150 Words Per Minute

Average Reader—250 Words Per Minute

Fast Reader—350 Words Per Minute

A student who consistently reads at an average or above-average rate (with satisfactory comprehension) is ready to advance to the next book in the series.

A column of Xs in the Comprehension Skills Profile indicates a specific comprehension weakness. Using the profile, you can assess trends in student performance and suggest remedial work if necessary.

When the Stars Shone in Harlem

On March 21, 1924, a dozen or so young, mostly unknown African American writers dined at the Civic Club in downtown Manhattan, New York. Several white editors and publishers were there as well. The dinner was the brainchild of an African American named Charles Johnson, a respected educator. He had founded *Opportunity* the year before. He hoped this magazine, a scholarly publication, would improve black-white relations in the United States. He also hoped his dinner would bring African American writers to the attention of the literary world. This event is considered the launching point of a literary movement called the Harlem Renaissance.

Harlem, in northern Manhattan, began drawing large numbers of African Americans perhaps 10 years into the twentieth century. By the 1920s, Harlem contained one of the largest communities of African Americans in the entire country.

The Renaissance, from the French word for "rebirth," was the name historians had given to a period of intense creativity in the mid-fourteenth to the sixteenth centuries. This movement began in Italy and spread throughout Europe. Its name captured the idea of the rebirth and flowering of culture that followed the Middle Ages.

Like its predecessor, the Harlem Renaissance was a rebirth of culture. In this case, it was African American culture and folk roots that were being revitalized in the arts. A little more than a year after the historic Civic Club dinner, Johnson and his magazine sponsored a literary-awards dinner. The attendees numbered 316 and included the shining lights of Harlem's literary community. Some, such as novelist Jean Toomer (*Cane*) and poet Charles McKay (*Harlem Shadows*), were already published and esteemed writers. Others shone brightly for a few years and then dropped from the literary scene, but a few stars who were honored that night with prizes have gone on to secure their places in literary history. These include the writer Zora Neale Hurston (*Their Eyes Were Watching God*) and the poets Countee Cullen (*Color*) and Langston Hughes (*The Weary Blues* and *The Dream Keeper*, which contains the often-reprinted "Dreams").

The creative rebirth in Harlem was short-lived. It ended in the mid-1930s, destroyed by the massive unemployment and financial turmoil of the Great Depression. The spirit of the Harlem Renaissance, however, lived on to inspire new generations of African American writers. The enduring works of its writers and poets continue to speak to people around the world.

Reading Time _____

Recalling Facts

1. The Harlem Renaissance was
   - ❏ a. a period in the mid-fourteenth century.
   - ❏ b. the name given to a 1920s American literary movement.
   - ❏ c. the creation of an African American educator named Charles Johnson.

2. Works produced during the Harlem Renaissance
   - ❏ a. were ignored by publishers.
   - ❏ b. focused on the African American experience.
   - ❏ c. were too narrowly focused to have a wide audience.

3. The term *renaissance* comes from the French word meaning
   - ❏ a. rebirth.
   - ❏ b. cultural roots.
   - ❏ c. revitalization.

4. At the 1925 awards dinner, two already published and esteemed attendees were
   - ❏ a. Jean Toomer and Charles McKay.
   - ❏ b. Langston Hughes and Jean Toomer.
   - ❏ c. Zora Neale Hurston and Countee Cullen.

5. *The Dream Keeper,* by Langston Hughes, is a
   - ❏ a. novel.
   - ❏ b. folktale.
   - ❏ c. collection of poems.

Understanding Ideas

6. The Harlem Renaissance was aptly named because
   - ❏ a. it took place exclusively in Harlem.
   - ❏ b. its writers considered themselves "reborn" in a religious sense.
   - ❏ c. like the Italian Renaissance, it was a burst of creativity inspired by its own rich past.

7. It is likely that one of Johnson's goals in giving his 1924 dinner was to
   - ❏ a. start a literary movement.
   - ❏ b. find a sponsor for his magazine.
   - ❏ c. get other African American writers published.

8. One can conclude that Johnson was
   - ❏ a. known and respected in African American and white literary circles.
   - ❏ b. known only to African American writers.
   - ❏ c. not well known to African Americans.

9. The author's attitude toward the writers of the Harlem Renaissance is best described as
   - ❏ a. neutral.
   - ❏ b. admiring.
   - ❏ c. skeptical.

10. It is fair to conclude that winning a literary prize
    - ❏ a. secures for the writer a place in literary history.
    - ❏ b. is an honor that may or may not indicate that the writer will achieve an enduring legacy.
    - ❏ c. probably means that the writer is well liked and respected.

Regina Anderson, an active member of the Harlem Renaissance community, called him the "poet laureate of Harlem." In dubbing Langston Hughes thus, Anderson proclaimed him the best and most representative of his locality and group. History seems to bear out her judgment. Thanks to copious translations, Hughes may well be the world's foremost interpreter of the African American experience.

Brought up by his mother and grandmother in the early 1900s, Hughes was often uprooted. He began creating poems, he would later confess, "mostly because when I felt bad, writing kept me from feeling worse." His poetic efforts commanded early attention, as evidenced by his election as class poet in grade school in Lincoln, Illinois. He published his first poem in 1921, when he was only 19 years old. Four years later, at the *Opportunity* awards dinner of 1925, his poem "The Weary Blues" garnered first place.

Hughes elevated himself to national attention, it is said, when he was a busboy in a Washington, D.C., hotel in the mid-1920s. Supposedly, he left three of his poems beside the plate of Vachel Lindsay, a highly regarded poet.

Weary Blues, a collection that includes his award-winning poem of the same name, was published in 1926 to critical success.

The power of his voice has made Langston Hughes one of the United States' premier poets.

1. **Recognizing Words in Context**

   Find the word *copious* in the passage. One definition below is closest to the meaning of that word. One definition has the opposite or nearly the opposite meaning. The remaining definition has a completely different meaning. Label the definitions C for *closest,* O for *opposite or nearly opposite,* and D for *different.*

   _____ a. scarce

   _____ b. abundant

   _____ c. prominent

2. **Distinguishing Fact from Opinion**

   Two of the statements below present *facts,* which can be proved. The other statement is an *opinion,* which expresses someone's thoughts or beliefs. Label the statements F for *fact* and O for *opinion.*

   _____ a. Regina Anderson called Hughes "the poet laureate of Harlem."

   _____ b. At the *Opportunity* awards dinner of 1925, Hughes's poem won first place.

   _____ c. Hughes is the best writer to come out of the Harlem Renaissance.

3. Keeping Events in Order

Number the statements below 1, 2, and 3 to show the order in which the events took place.

_____ a. Hughes won a prize at the *Opportunity* awards dinner.

_____ b. Hughes published his first poem.

_____ c. Hughes received critical acclaim for *Weary Blues.*

4. Making Correct Inferences

Two of the statements below are correct *inferences,* or reasonable guesses. They are based on information in the passage. The other statement is an incorrect, or faulty, inference. Label the statements C for *correct* inference and F for *faulty* inference.

_____ a. People around Hughes recognized that he had talent.

_____ b. Even in grade school, people knew that Hughes would go on to become a famous poet someday.

_____ c. The discovery of Hughes may or may not have been the result of his experience with Vachel Lindsay.

5. Understanding Main Ideas

One of the statements below expresses the main idea of the passage. One statement is too general, or too broad. The other explains only part of the passage; it is too narrow. Label the statements M for *main idea,* B for *too broad,* and N for *too narrow.*

_____ a. The Harlem Renaissance produced many talented writers, including Langston Hughes.

_____ b. Langston Hughes began writing poetry at an early age.

_____ c. Langston Hughes, an African American writer of the Harlem Renaissance, is one of America's premier poets.

Correct Answers, Part A _____

Correct Answers, Part B _____

Total Correct Answers _____

The Fishing Industry of Nova Scotia

Fishing is perhaps the oldest industry in Nova Scotia, dating back to the 1500s, when European fishermen caught cod in the surrounding ocean and then dried them on those shores. Despite dangers to seafarers—such as rough seas, submerged rocks, and fog—Europeans began settling in Nova Scotia in the 1600s. For centuries, cod fishing formed the basis of Nova Scotia's international trade. Merchants sold dried, salted cod in Europe, the West Indies, and elsewhere.

In the 1700s, the government started building lighthouses to guide ships safely to port. The lighthouses emitted a beacon of light that warned mariners of hazards and served as signposts to tell sailors where they were. Many lighthouses had foghorns, whose loud boom cut through fog when light could not. Although lighthouses did not prevent all shipwrecks, they saved many fishing fleets from disaster.

With the advent of refrigeration and motorized ships, Nova Scotia fishers responded to customer demands for fresh and frozen seafood. Better equipment and new fishing technology, such as sonar to locate fish, also enabled fishing fleets to catch more fish.

However, in the mid-1900s, certain species of fish, including cod and haddock, declined in number and size. Overfishing, or the catching of too many fish, appeared to be one factor causing this decline. Since that time, the Canadian government has extended its fishing zone to 200 nautical miles in order to exclude foreign vessels from fishing there. It has also limited catches and banned fishing in certain areas and during certain times of the year. These measures may help, but it may take years before the numbers of slowly maturing fish, such as cod, increase significantly.

Today, aquaculture, or raising fish and shellfish on "farms," is part of the fishing industry. Species such as Atlantic salmon, rainbow trout, sea scallops, and oysters are farm raised. Lobster, scallop, crab, and shrimp each bring in more money to the fishing industry than any one kind of fish. Yet, as recently as 2000, of all fish caught, cod and haddock were the most profitable for the fishing industry, although other fish were more plentiful.

The availability of seafood has a direct impact on the livelihood of thousands of people employed in various aspects of the fishing industry, including fishing and fish processing. With fishing fleets catching fewer fish, many people have lost jobs. Others worry about what will happen if fish, such as cod, do not make a comeback.

Reading Time _____

Recalling Facts

1. For centuries, the basis of Nova Scotia's international trade was
   - ❑ a. lobster.
   - ❑ b. cod fishing.
   - ❑ c. fish processing.

2. Better equipment and new fishing technology meant that
   - ❑ a. a fishing fleet could catch more fish.
   - ❑ b. salt cod became the focus of the fishing industry.
   - ❑ c. refrigeration and motorized ships no longer were needed.

3. As recently as 2000, of all fish caught, cod and haddock were
   - ❑ a. the most plentiful.
   - ❑ b. the least likely to sell.
   - ❑ c. the most profitable for the fishing industry.

4. Today, aquaculture is part of
   - ❑ a. fish processing.
   - ❑ b. the fishing industry.
   - ❑ c. a motorized sailing ship.

5. Lobster, scallop, crab, and shrimp each bring in
   - ❑ a. the same amount of money as cod.
   - ❑ b. less money than any one kind of fish.
   - ❑ c. more money than any one kind of fish.

Understanding Ideas

6. One can conclude from the passage that, for several centuries,
   - ❑ a. cod were farm raised.
   - ❑ b. overfishing of cod was not a problem.
   - ❑ c. cod were the most plentiful fish off the coast of Nova Scotia.

7. Although the short-term result of better equipment and technology was increased efficiency, the long-term result presented
   - ❑ a. a danger to cod and haddock populations.
   - ❑ b. opportunities for Canadian fishers to catch more cod and haddock.
   - ❑ c. increased fishing of cod and haddock for foreign fleets near Nova Scotia.

8. It is likely that continued overfishing will cause
   - ❑ a. more salt cod to be sold.
   - ❑ b. fishing fleets to increase in size.
   - ❑ c. more people in the fishing industry to lose their jobs.

9. One can infer from the passage that fishing continues to be
   - ❑ a. a growing industry in Nova Scotia.
   - ❑ b. unimportant to Nova Scotia's economy.
   - ❑ c. an important part of Nova Scotia's economy.

10. One can infer from the passage that aquaculture will probably
    - ❑ a. become outdated soon.
    - ❑ b. replace lighthouses soon.
    - ❑ c. become an increasingly important part of the fishing industry.

Tidal Action in the Bay of Fundy

The Bay of Fundy is a long extension of the Atlantic Ocean between the Canadian provinces of New Brunswick and Nova Scotia. A multiplicity of creatures can be found in the Bay of Fundy. Algae grow on mud flats, and minuscule organisms called plankton flourish in the water. Krill, small shrimplike creatures, become food for birds and migrating whales— including North Atlantic right whales—that feed in the bay. Fish and crustaceans, such as lobsters, are also a part of the bay's diverse ecosystem, created in part by the ocean tides that agitate the waters, bringing food from the bottom to the surface of the bay and creating mud flats and salt marshes where animals and plants thrive.

The tides in the Bay of Fundy are the highest in the world, attaining heights greater than 50 feet. The funnel shape and depth of the bay contribute to creating these enormous tides. At the wide end of the bay, the incoming tide may be about 11 feet high, but it increases in height as it progresses into the narrowing and increasingly shallow bay, eventually becoming a wall of water that forces rivers to reverse their seaward flow and rush inland. In places, the tides have carved underground caves into the rocky coastline or sculpted sandstone into towering shapes and arches.

1. **Recognizing Words in Context**

   Find the word *multiplicity* in the passage. One definition below is closest to the meaning of that word. One definition has the opposite or nearly the opposite meaning. The remaining definition has a completely different meaning. Label the definitions C for *closest*, O for *opposite or nearly opposite*, and D for *different*.

   _____ a. municipality

   _____ b. limited number

   _____ c. abundance

2. **Distinguishing Fact from Opinion**

   Two of the statements below present *facts*, which can be proved. The other statement is an *opinion*, which expresses someone's thoughts or beliefs. Label the statements F for *fact* and O for *opinion*.

   _____ a. The tides sculpt sandstone into the most beautiful shapes.

   _____ b. The tides in the Bay of Fundy are the highest in the world.

   _____ c. Migrating whales feed in the bay.

3. **Keeping Events in Order**

Number the statements below 1, 2, and 3 to show the order in which the events took place.

_____ a. The tide becomes a wall of water.

_____ b. The incoming tide reaches the wide end of the Bay of Fundy.

_____ c. The tide increases in height as it moves into the narrowing bay.

4. **Making Correct Inferences**

Two of the statements below are correct *inferences,* or reasonable guesses. They are based on information in the passage. The other statement is an incorrect, or faulty, inference. Label the statements C for *correct* inference and F for *faulty* inference.

_____ a. The tides will eventually destroy the bottom of the ocean.

_____ b. The tides in the Bay of Fundy are forceful.

_____ c. The tides have the potential to change the ecosystem.

5. **Understanding Main Ideas**

One of the statements below expresses the main idea of the passage. One statement is too general, or too broad. The other explains only part of the passage; it is too narrow. Label the statements M for *main idea,* B for *too broad,* and N for *too narrow.*

_____ a. Many animals feed in the Bay of Fundy.

_____ b. The changes brought about by tidal waters affect the surrounding ecosystems.

_____ c. Ocean tides help to shape the Bay of Fundy's coast and to create the bay's ecosystem.

Correct Answers, Part A _____

Correct Answers, Part B _____

Total Correct Answers _____

Connecting Two Oceans

In 1904 the United States began a major engineering project in Panama: to connect the Atlantic Ocean to the Pacific Ocean. For centuries people had dreamed of a water route through Central America that would shorten the journey from one ocean to the other. With the completion of the Panama Canal, that dream became reality.

National defense and a desire to maintain naval supremacy were two reasons that leaders of the United States wanted to build the Panama Canal. In 1898, during the Spanish-American War, the U.S. Navy sent a ship from San Francisco to Cuba. The ship traveled nearly 13 thousand miles because it had to sail around South America. Had the Panama Canal existed, the journey would have been about 46 hundred miles. With a canal, ships could also have transported passengers and goods between oceans much more quickly and, as a result, more cheaply.

Although many reasons existed for building the Panama Canal, the work itself was fraught with danger. The tropical climate of Panama was an ideal breeding ground for poisonous snakes, scorpions, ticks, spiders, rats, and other pests. Diseases such as malaria, smallpox, pneumonia, tuberculosis, and dysentery plagued workers, killing many. During the first year of work, squalid living conditions and a poor diet also sickened many workers.

Swamplands and rocky terrain also helped to make building the canal hard work. Workers used heavy machines to cut away and move tons of dirt. They worked 10 hours a day, at least six days a week, in both dry and rainy seasons. Landslides claimed lives, and some workers drowned in floods. Workers used dynamite to blast passageways, such as the nine-mile-long Culebra Cut, through mountains. They built a dam across the Chagres River as well as locks on the canal. (A lock is a water-filled chamber that can raise or lower ships from one level of a waterway to another.) Many lost lives or limbs in blasting accidents.

Many people quit their jobs because of the risks and hardships they experienced. However, many others came to Panama eager to work. After the first year, living conditions improved dramatically. A new chief engineer made sure that workers had clean housing, plumbing, hospitals, schools, and healthful food.

By the time the canal opened in 1914, the more than 50-mile-long project had cost the United States more than $350 million and employed tens of thousands of people from around the world.

Reading Time _____

Recalling Facts

1. When the Panama Canal was completed,
   - ❏ a. port cities along the coasts of South America celebrated.
   - ❏ b. merchants in Europe and Asia anticipated an increase in costs and shipping.
   - ❏ c. the dream of connecting the Atlantic and Pacific through Central America became a reality.

2. With a canal, ships could transport passengers between oceans
   - ❏ a. in a couple of hours.
   - ❏ b. much more quickly and cheaply.
   - ❏ c. more expensively but in a much shorter time.

3. The tropical climate of Panama, which produced lush vegetation and exotic animals,
   - ❏ a. made it a canal worker's paradise.
   - ❏ b. also bred pests and diseases.
   - ❏ c. was the principal reason for locating the canal there.

4. The high sickness rate among canal workers during the first year was the result of
   - ❏ a. unhealthful food.
   - ❏ b. unsanitary living conditions and poor diet.
   - ❏ c. workers' lack of experience in the job and in a hot climate.

5. Many people quit their jobs at the canal because
   - ❏ a. of the risks and hardships involved.
   - ❏ b. they had earned all the money they needed.
   - ❏ c. there were better opportunities in their home countries.

Understanding Ideas

6. It is probable that the Panama Canal was not built earlier because
   - ❏ a. Panama would not allow foreigners to enter.
   - ❏ b. engineering and health challenges exceeded capabilities.
   - ❏ c. other countries in Central America wanted to be the site.

7. It is likely that many people worked to build the Panama Canal because they
   - ❏ a. sought adventure.
   - ❏ b. needed the money.
   - ❏ c. wanted to solve the engineering problems posed by the project.

8. One can infer from the passage that for many Panama Canal workers
   - ❏ a. the benefits outweighed the dangers.
   - ❏ b. there were few physical risks involved.
   - ❏ c. schools were the main benefit.

9. One can conclude from the passage that the new chief engineer improved living conditions for workers because
   - ❏ a. workers threatened to strike if he did not.
   - ❏ b. he believed that many deaths caused by disease could be prevented.
   - ❏ c. he did not want worker housing overrun by dangerous pests.

10. It is probable that improving living conditions
    - ❏ a. was more expensive in the long run.
    - ❏ b. led to improved productivity.
    - ❏ c. was prompted by international media attention.

Fighting Yellow Fever in Panama

Most experts think that tropical diseases were the greatest hazard to those who built the Panama Canal. During the French's attempt at the project in the 1880s, thousands of workers died from mosquito-borne diseases such as yellow fever.

In 1904, before construction began, the canal commission hired Colonel William C. Gorgas, an American doctor, to improve health and sanitation in the Canal Zone. Gorgas, an expert on tropical diseases, previously had led the team that wiped out yellow fever in Havana, Cuba.

Gorgas was determined to eliminate breeding sites of the mosquitoes that carried yellow fever. In Havana he learned the habits of the species. The female lays her eggs in clean, standing water, such as in grain barrels or wells. Gorgas's staff covered open containers of fresh water with lids, screens, or a thin layer of oil. The oil smothered mosquito larvae. This kept the females from laying eggs there.

Gorgas also devised methods to keep people from being bitten by mosquitoes. Workers installed screens on doors and windows. Each morning, workers set forth to exterminate mosquitoes. Going from building to building, they sealed doors and windows with newspaper. Then they used insecticides inside each building.

By 1906 yellow fever in the Canal Zone had been eradicated.

1. Recognizing Words in Context

Find the word *eliminate* in the passage. One definition below is closest to the meaning of that word. One definition has the opposite or nearly the opposite meaning. The remaining definition has a completely different meaning. Label the definitions C for *closest*, O for *opposite or nearly opposite*, and D for *different*.

_____ a. foster

_____ b. ignore

_____ c. destroy

2. Distinguishing Fact from Opinion

Two of the statements below present *facts*, which can be proved. The other statement is an *opinion*, which expresses someone's thoughts or beliefs. Label the statements F for *fact* and O for *opinion*.

_____ a. Colonel William C. Gorgas helped wipe out yellow fever in Havana, Cuba.

_____ b. Tropical diseases were the greatest hazards to those who built the Panama Canal.

_____ c. Oil smothered mosquito larvae.

3. **Keeping Events in Order**

   Number the statements below 1, 2, and 3 to show the order in which the events took place.

   _____ a. Gorgas won the fight to eradicate yellow fever.

   _____ b. The canal commission hired Gorgas to improve health and sanitation in the Canal Zone.

   _____ c. Gorgas, an expert in tropical diseases, learned the habits of the species of mosquitoes that carried the yellow fever virus.

4. **Making Correct Inferences**

   Two of the statements below are correct *inferences,* or reasonable guesses. They are based on information in the passage. The other statement is an incorrect, or faulty, inference. Label the statements C for *correct* inference and F for *faulty* inference.

   _____ a. Gorgas determined that the most efficient way to eliminate the yellow fever virus was to eliminate the means by which it was transmitted to human beings.

   _____ b. Controlling the mosquito population requires a variety of strategic actions.

   _____ c. Mosquito-borne diseases are no longer a problem.

5. **Understanding Main Ideas**

   One of the statements below expresses the main idea of the passage. One statement is too general, or too broad. The other explains only part of the passage; it is too narrow. Label the statements M for *main idea,* B for *too broad,* and N for *too narrow.*

   _____ a. Tropical disease experts study mosquitoes and their transmission of deadly diseases.

   _____ b. William C. Gorgas gained experience eliminating yellow fever by helping to wipe it out in Cuba.

   _____ c. William C. Gorgas used his expertise to eradicate yellow fever in the Panama Canal Zone.

Correct Answers, Part A _____

Correct Answers, Part B _____

Total Correct Answers _____

Powerful First Ladies

The title "First Lady of the United States" is given to the wife of the nation's president. The duties of most First Ladies have included arranging and attending social functions, such as state dinners. As the president's wife, the First Lady is in a highly visible position. Therefore, her behavior can make her a role model. She can change people's thinking by supporting a favorite cause. The First Lady also has access to influential people, including the president. Many First Ladies have used their position and skills to draw attention to, and change, social and other policies, and sometimes events have forced a First Lady to take a prominent role in leading the country.

First Lady Edith Wilson assumed many of her husband's duties after a stroke in 1919 left Woodrow Wilson weak and partly paralyzed. For many months she decided who could see him, determined which issues required his attention, and passed on other matters to members of his staff. Some people called her the Secret President, and many praised her for her judgment.

After polio limited her husband's mobility, Eleanor Roosevelt worked tirelessly on his behalf. Franklin Delano Roosevelt began his presidency during the Great Depression. Both he and his wife cared deeply about helping the unemployed and providing relief for the needy. As First Lady, she went places he could not go, traveling widely and reporting to him what she saw and heard. She visited protesting war veterans, coal miners in Appalachia, slum dwellers, and sharecroppers; she also inspected government relief projects. During World War II she traveled abroad as America's goodwill ambassador.

Believing that it was vital to inform the public about the president's and her own thoughts and actions, Eleanor Roosevelt was the first presidential wife to hold press conferences. As First Lady, she gave lectures and radio talks and wrote articles. She began writing a newspaper column titled "My Day," which shared her views on social, political, and other issues. Thousands of people wrote to her, asking for help. When she could not answer a letter personally, she forwarded it to the appropriate government agency to answer.

Eleanor Roosevelt was an outspoken supporter of civil rights and worked to end prejudice. She urged women to be politically active and supported programs to aid jobless women. As a result of her influence, there were more women than ever before working in a president's administration.

Reading Time _____

Recalling Facts

1. A First Lady can change people's thinking by
   - ❏ a. attending social functions.
   - ❏ b. supporting a favorite cause.
   - ❏ c. having an understanding of world affairs.

2. Edith Wilson assumed many of her husband's duties
   - ❏ a. because he was so busy.
   - ❏ b. when he went away on trips.
   - ❏ c. after a stroke left him weak and partly paralyzed.

3. Some people called Edith Wilson
   - ❏ a. the Second Wilson.
   - ❏ b. the Secret President.
   - ❏ c. Mrs. E. W. President.

4. Eleanor Roosevelt was the first presidential wife to
   - ❏ a. work.
   - ❏ b. travel abroad.
   - ❏ c. hold press conferences.

5. According to the passage, as a result of Eleanor Roosevelt's influence, more women than ever
   - ❏ a. were unemployed.
   - ❏ b. worked in a president's administration.
   - ❏ c. were involved in social-advocacy work in their hometowns.

Understanding Ideas

6. One can infer that one reason the First Lady is powerful is that she
   - ❏ a. attends state dinners.
   - ❏ b. can influence the president's actions.
   - ❏ c. has experience and advanced degrees that others do not.

7. Edith Wilson and Eleanor Roosevelt both
   - ❏ a. aided their husbands.
   - ❏ b. championed special causes.
   - ❏ c. wrote articles in newspapers that influenced the public.

8. In contrast to Eleanor Roosevelt, Edith Wilson
   - ❏ a. was outspoken on social issues.
   - ❏ b. assumed many of her husband's duties.
   - ❏ c. traveled widely around the globe.

9. One can infer that people wrote to Eleanor Roosevelt for help because
   - ❏ a. she was wealthy.
   - ❏ b. she was outspoken.
   - ❏ c. they believed that she would help them.

10. One can conclude that one cause Eleanor Roosevelt supported was
    - ❏ a. clean air.
    - ❏ b. women's rights.
    - ❏ c. national health care.

At the time of her death in 1994, Jacqueline Kennedy Onassis, widow of shipping magnate Aristotle Onassis, had had a long career in publishing. To many people, however, she remained Jackie, the stylish young wife of President John F. Kennedy.

During her time as First Lady, many women considered her their role model. They emulated her, dressing as she dressed. She charmed not only the American public but also people around the world. In France she was the interpreter between her husband and President Charles de Gaulle. She impressed de Gaulle with her knowledge of France and its language.

As First Lady, Jacqueline Kennedy took on a special project: restoring the White House to reflect the nation's history and arts. Before moving into the presidential residence in 1961, she researched its history. Then she established the White House Historical Association to raise funds for her project. In February 1962 she broadcast a televised tour of the newly restored White House, which about one-third of the American public watched.

Despite her popularity, Jacqueline Kennedy was a private person who cherished her time with her children and her husband. Her courage after her husband's assassination in 1963 earned her the respect of people throughout the world.

1. **Recognizing Words in Context**

   Find the word *emulated* in the passage. One definition below is closest to the meaning of that word. One definition has the opposite or nearly the opposite meaning. The remaining definition has a completely different meaning. Label the definitions C for *closest*, O for *opposite or nearly opposite*, and D for *different*.

   _____ a. informed

   _____ b. opposed

   _____ c. imitated

2. **Distinguishing Fact from Opinion**

   Two of the statements below present *facts*, which can be proved. The other statement is an *opinion*, which expresses someone's thoughts or beliefs. Label the statements F for *fact* and O for *opinion*.

   _____ a. Kennedy's special project was restoring the White House.

   _____ b. About one-third of the American public watched the televised tour of the White House.

   _____ c. Kennedy was the most stylish of all First Ladies.

3. **Keeping Events in Order**

Number the statements below 1, 2, and 3 to show the order in which the events took place.

_____ a. Jacqueline Kennedy researched the history of the White House.

_____ b. A tour of the White House was televised.

_____ c. The White House Historical Association was established.

4. **Making Correct Inferences**

Two of the statements below are correct *inferences,* or reasonable guesses. They are based on information in the passage. The other statement is an incorrect, or faulty, inference. Label the statements C for *correct* inference and F for *faulty* inference.

_____ a. Jacqueline Kennedy worked in publishing to gain publicity.

_____ b. Many women aspired to be like Jacqueline Kennedy because they admired her.

_____ c. Jacqueline Kennedy was intelligent.

5. **Understanding Main Ideas**

One of the statements below expresses the main idea of the passage. One statement is too general, or too broad. The other explains only part of the passage; it is too narrow. Label the statements M for *main idea,* B for *too broad,* and N for *too narrow.*

_____ a. Jacqueline Kennedy was the wife of President John F. Kennedy.

_____ b. Many First Ladies, such as Jacqueline Kennedy Onassis, were of great interest to the American public.

_____ c. Jacqueline Kennedy Onassis was a former First Lady who charmed and impressed others with her style, knowledge, and courage.

Correct Answers, Part A _____

Correct Answers, Part B _____

Total Correct Answers _____

The Invention of the Wheel

When the first wheel was created some 6 thousand years ago, one could say that it started history "rolling." The facts concerning its invention, however, are murky.

Historians agree that the wheel originated in Mesopotamia, the region in the Middle East that follows the curve of the Tigris and Euphrates Rivers. This is the area known as the Fertile Crescent. To many, it is the birthplace of civilization, the place where farming became systematic and rural settlements evolved into busy cities and economic centers. At some point during the fourth millennium B.C., some person, or some group of people, thought of the idea of placing round logs under a sledge, a conveyance similar to a sled. As they (or their animals) pulled on the sledge, the logs rolled forward, moving the load more quickly and easily.

It is an enormous technological jump, however, from rolling a sledge over logs to pulling a platform or box that has been secured over wheels. Written language did not yet exist, and in the absence of any concrete historical record, the circumstances surrounding this transition are purely a subject of speculation.

Artifacts from about 3,000 B.C. show pictures of wheeled vehicles. This indicates that the technology must have been fairly well established by then. The earliest wheels appear to have been made from three flat boards pegged together and cut into a circle. The ancient Mesopotamians already knew how to make an accurate circle, using a hinged compass similar to ones used today in a geometry class. This instrument had been invented in Mesopotamia about a thousand years earlier.

Wouldn't it have been more logical, however, simply to cut a disk from one of those roller-logs? Not in Mesopotamia, where there were few forests and trees tended to be small and slender. Their trunks were suitable for use as rollers but not nearly large enough in diameter to produce slabs that would function as wheels. Wheels were still constructed from planks, even in civilizations where trees of large circumference were commonly found. As a cross-section of a tree trunk dries, cracks quickly open from the center to the edge. Such a "wheel" of wood would disintegrate under stress.

Subsequent developments in wheel technology included a lighter wheel with spokes, the use of an iron ring as a "tire" to make a wheel more durable, and hinged axles that allowed wheels to rotate at different speeds.

Reading Time _____

Recalling Facts

1. The wheel probably originated
   - ❑ a. in Egypt.
   - ❑ b. in Mesopotamia about 6 thousand years ago.
   - ❑ c. where trees of large circumference were common.

2. The first wheels were
   - ❑ a. wrapped in iron.
   - ❑ b. disks cut from tree trunks.
   - ❑ c. cut from flat boards pegged together.

3. When the wheel was invented,
   - ❑ a. written language did not yet exist.
   - ❑ b. the compass had not yet been invented.
   - ❑ c. settlers had not yet arrived in the Fertile Crescent.

4. Subsequent developments in wheel technology included
   - ❑ a. using a compass as a guide when cutting out an accurate circle.
   - ❑ b. placing round logs underneath a sledge as rollers.
   - ❑ c. using hinged axles that allowed wheels to rotate at different speeds.

5. A cross-section of a tree trunk would not have made a good wheel because it would have
   - ❑ a. been very heavy.
   - ❑ b. been a perfect circle.
   - ❑ c. cracked as the wood dried and broke apart when used.

Understanding Ideas

6. The wheel was invented in the Fertile Crescent probably because
   - ❑ a. traveling by foot was especially difficult there.
   - ❑ b. this region had the best trees for wheel making.
   - ❑ c. this area was the site of many important technological and social advances.

7. Before a successful wheel was made from pegged boards, it is likely that someone experimented with
   - ❑ a. casting iron into disks.
   - ❑ b. shaping stones into disks.
   - ❑ c. cutting a disk from a tree trunk.

8. From the passage, one can conclude that the inventors of the wheel had to discover or know about the
   - ❑ a. condition of existing roads.
   - ❑ b. physical properties of wood.
   - ❑ c. distances to be traveled.

9. Compared with using logs as rollers, the wheel was a technological leap because
   - ❑ a. wood has material limitations.
   - ❑ b. it required combining several components into one mechanism.
   - ❑ c. it would prove to have a major impact on the course of history.

10. Which of the following sentences best expresses the main idea?
    - ❑ a. The wheel made it possible to carry heavy loads for long distances.
    - ❑ b. Among artifacts from about 3000 B.C. are pictures of wheeled vehicles.
    - ❑ c. The wheel originated about 6,000 years ago in Mesopotamia.

Sumerian Chariots: The First Vehicles of War

The chariot looks a little like a four-wheeled cart. It is pulled by four long-eared animals, probably onagers or some other ancient species of donkey. The wheels on the chariot are solid, not spoked like a modern wheel.

This earliest known depiction of a chariot was found in the late 1920s. Excavated from a grave in the state of Sumer in southern Mesopotamia (modern-day Iraq), an oblong object called the "standard of Ur," probably created about 2,500 B.C., was found. On this boxlike object was a colorful mosaic of bits of shell, red limestone, and blue lapis lazuli. Its function is obscure, however. Although it was originally thought to be a symbol or standard held aloft in parades, some scholars now believe that it may have been the sounding box of a musical instrument.

Evidence suggests that the wheel was invented in Mesopotamia toward the end of the fourth millennium B.C. The warlike Sumerians, therefore, were probably the first to adapt wheeled vehicles to military use. The early chariots were heavy and comparatively slow. They were difficult to maneuver and produced a bumpy ride that made accurate use of an arrow or a spear almost impossible. In fact, the chariots were probably first used to crash through enemy lines and create openings for soldiers running behind on foot.

1. **Recognizing Words in Context**

   Find the word *obscure* in the passage. One definition below is closest to the meaning of that word. One definition has the opposite or nearly the opposite meaning. The remaining definition has a completely different meaning. Label the definitions C for *closest*, O for *opposite or nearly opposite,* and D for *different*.

   _____ a. extravagant

   _____ b unclear

   _____ c. obvious

2. **Distinguishing Fact from Opinion**

   Two of the statements below present *facts,* which can be proved. The other statement is an *opinion,* which expresses someone's thoughts or beliefs. Label the statements F for *fact* and O for *opinion*.

   _____ a. The first Sumerian chariots had four wheels.

   _____ b. The standard of Ur was the sounding box of a musical instrument.

   _____ c. Chariots were used in war to crash through the enemy line.

3. Keeping Events in Order

Number the statements below 1, 2, and 3 to show the order in which the events took place.

_____ a. Various objects were excavated from a grave in Sumer.

_____ b. Wheeled vehicles came into use in Sumer.

_____ c. The standard of Ur was decorated with mosaics of chariots.

4. Making Correct Inferences

Two of the statements below are correct *inferences*, or reasonable guesses. They are based on information in the passage. The other statement is an incorrect, or faulty, inference. Label the statements C for *correct* inference and F for *faulty* inference.

_____ a. One can learn about life in ancient Sumer by examining the decorations on various objects.

_____ b. The wheel was invented for use in war.

_____ c. A standard could also take the form of a flag or a banner.

5. Understanding Main Ideas

One of the statements below expresses the main idea of the passage. One statement is too general, or too broad. The other explains only part of the passage; it is too narrow. Label the statements M for *main idea*, B for *too broad*, and N for *too narrow*.

_____ a. Many forms of transportation were invented over the course of history.

_____ b. In ancient times, the Sumerians used chariots to crash through the enemy lines.

_____ c. An ancient mosaic decoration suggests that the Sumerians were probably the first to use chariots.

Correct Answers, Part A _____

Correct Answers, Part B _____

Total Correct Answers _____

Women's Role in Nazi Germany

In 1933 Adolf Hitler, leader of the Nazi party, gained control of the German government and declared himself *fuhrer*, or leader. Hitler believed that women should be mothers and housewives and that men should be workers and soldiers. He considered it a woman's duty to produce as many children as possible to make Germany more powerful. To coerce women and men into their distinct roles, the Nazis passed laws, used propaganda, and resorted to other tactics.

The Law for the Encouragement of Marriage made getting married and having children appealing to people. This law made loans available to newly married couples. A couple that had four children did not have to repay the loan. Funds for these loans were provided by heavy taxes on childless couples and single men.

Posters advertising the ideal German family showed women caring for children and men going to work. One Nazi slogan described a woman's life as church, children, and cooking. A woman who had four or more children received a medal called the Mother's Cross every year on August 12, the birthday of Hitler's mother.

One of the regime's primary goals was to create loyal Nazis. Textbooks were rewritten to include the Nazi version of German history. Teachers were required to teach children Nazi beliefs. In school, girls were taught the skills they needed to be good housewives and mothers. Meanwhile, boys received a broad education, studying math, science, boxing, and other subjects that would make them good workers and soldiers.

Youth organizations also groomed children for their adult roles. Groups for girls reinforced the belief that girls should be healthy and physically fit for bearing children. Girls participated in sports for strength, and they learned housekeeping skills.

Because he believed that women were inferior to men, Hitler mandated that the worlds of men and women should remain separate. He declared women—as too emotional to be logical and objective—ineligible for jury duty. In one speech, he said that he detested women who dabbled in politics. To him government was a masculine field for which women were unsuited.

The Nazis gradually required married women to stop working and replaced them with men, although unmarried women were still permitted to work. However, a shortage of skilled workers caused the Nazis to pass a law requiring women to spend a year working.

Reading Time _____

Recalling Facts

1. Hitler believed that women should be
   - ❑ a. workers and soldiers.
   - ❑ b. politicians and leaders.
   - ❑ c. housewives and mothers.

2. Hitler thought it a German woman's duty to
   - ❑ a. produce as many children as possible.
   - ❑ b. join the workforce and lead new industries.
   - ❑ c. become a soldier but take care of administrative tasks.

3. Women who had four or more children received a
   - ❑ a. fine.
   - ❑ b. medal.
   - ❑ c. diploma.

4. Tactics used by Hitler to urge women to fulfill their roles as Nazis included
   - ❑ a. requiring girls to be physically fit and training women as soldiers.
   - ❑ b. giving rewards to the brightest students and promoting women in the workforce.
   - ❑ c. teaching Nazi beliefs to girls and removing married women from the workforce.

5. The Nazis gradually required married women to
   - ❑ a. stop working.
   - ❑ b. become soldiers.
   - ❑ c. have more children.

Understanding Ideas

6. One can conclude from the passage that girls received a limited education in order to
   - ❑ a. be efficient government workers.
   - ❑ b. exclude them from professional careers.
   - ❑ c. prepare them for whatever work they chose to do.

7. Before the Nazis governed Germany, it is likely that girls received
   - ❑ a. a better education.
   - ❑ b. a poorer education.
   - ❑ c. the same quality education.

8. In the long run, Hitler's attempt to keep women at home turned out to be
   - ❑ a. impractical for Germany.
   - ❑ b. beneficial to Germany's war effort.
   - ❑ c. a model for other European nations.

9. One can conclude from the passage that Hitler
   - ❑ a. surrounded himself with female advisors.
   - ❑ b. appointed an equal number of male and female government officials.
   - ❑ c. did not appoint women to positions of power within the Nazi government.

10. One can conclude from the passage that Hitler
    - ❑ a. increased women's rights.
    - ❑ b. deprived women of many rights.
    - ❑ c. thought women were more important than men.

Dr. Gerda Lerner: Putting Women into History

As a Jewish teenager in Austria, Gerda Lerner experienced the Nazis' rise to power. In 1938 Adolf Hitler announced the union of Austria and Germany. Nazis began terrorizing Jews, and Lerner fled to the United States.

Her experiences as a Jew and an immigrant made her realize that she was an outsider, and she knew that people often mistreated outsiders. Even as a child, Lerner was bothered by people's treating others badly. She wanted the world to reflect her sense of justice. In the United States, she protested acts that threatened people's rights and worked to improve people's lives.

In 1958, when her youngest child was 16, Lerner returned to school. In 1966 she earned a Ph.D. from Columbia University. There she noticed a dearth of women in the history books and questioned their absence. Her professors implied that women were absent because they had not contributed to history. Lerner knew that this was wrong because women had made notable achievements in many fields. Taking action, Lerner challenged commonly held notions about the impact of women in history. As a professor and distinguished scholar, she wrote books about women's achievements, started the nation's first graduate program in women's history, and proved that women are powerful—that they do have voices and that their contributions belong in history.

1. **Recognizing Words in Context**

Find the word *dearth* in the passage. One definition below is closest to the meaning of that word. One definition has the opposite or nearly the opposite meaning. The remaining definition has a completely different meaning. Label the definitions C for *closest*, O for *opposite or nearly opposite*, and D for *different*.

_____ a. overabundance

_____ b. lack

_____ c. death

2. **Distinguishing Fact from Opinion**

Two of the statements below present *facts*, which can be proved. The other statement is an *opinion*, which expresses someone's thoughts or beliefs. Label the statements F for *fact* and O for *opinion*.

_____ a. It is unfair that women's role in history has been so undermined.

_____ b. Gerda Lerner and other women achieved distinction in many fields.

_____ c. Gerda Lerner wrote books about women's accomplishments.

3. Keeping Events in Order

Number the statements below 1, 2, and 3 to show the order in which the events took place.

_____ a. Lerner questioned the absence of women in history books.

_____ b. Lerner challenged assumptions about women's importance in history.

_____ c. Lerner returned to school.

4. Making Correct Inferences

Two of the statements below are correct *inferences*, or reasonable guesses. They are based on information in the passage. The other statement is an incorrect, or faulty, inference. Label the statements C for *correct* inference and F for *faulty* inference.

_____ a. Lerner's life experiences influenced her career.

_____ b. Lerner is a pioneer in the field of women's history.

_____ c. Lerner thought women were superior to men.

5. Understanding Main Ideas

One of the statements below expresses the main idea of the passage. One statement is too general, or too broad. The other explains only part of the passage; it is too narrow. Label the statements M for *main idea*, B for *too broad*, and N for *too narrow*.

_____ a. Many immigrants have made valuable contributions to society, but too often little is known about them.

_____ b. As a result of her life experiences and her sense of justice, Gerda Lerner worked to have women represented in history.

_____ c. Gerda Lerner created the nation's first graduate program in women's history.

Correct Answers, Part A _____

Correct Answers, Part B _____

Total Correct Answers _____

7 A Cambodia's Khmer Civilization: The Angkor Period

The civilization of the ancient Khmer in Cambodia can be divided into three periods: pre-Angkor (before 802), Angkor (from 802 to 1431), and post-Angkor (after 1431). The pre-Angkor period included involvement in sea trade. Merchants who followed trade routes between the Middle East and China exposed the early Khmer to Hinduism and Buddhism. These two religions greatly influenced the Khmer civilization.

In 802 Jayavarman II proclaimed himself the sole ruler of Cambodia and identified himself with the Hindu god Shiva. In so doing, he established the Angkor kingdom and a king-god relationship that future rulers would follow. During the Angkor period, rulers had temples built to honor themselves and their chosen gods.

Several capital cities also were built during this time, many in the area of Angkor, in northwestern Cambodia. The cities attracted both foreigners and locals, many of whom waited at the royal palace for an audience with the king. At the marketplace, vendors displayed their products. Throngs of people milled about, some carrying goods on their heads and others riding horses, while oxcarts trundled through the streets.

Rulers also ordered the building of reservoirs and canals to provide water during the dry season. Today people still use West Baray, one of the major reservoirs of the Angkor period. Workers erected huge earth walls, called dikes, to create this reservoir. Thanks to effective irrigation systems, farmers eventually could grow as many as four rice crops per year. People stored their rice in covered woven baskets and cooked it in earthen pots. A Chinese visitor to the region wrote that people used their fingers to eat the rice because it was sticky.

Fish were plentiful too. People cast their nets from boats and hauled up carp, gudgeons, and other freshwater fish. Sometimes they hunted crocodiles for meat.

During the Angkor period, the Khmer empire attained its greatest size, expanding through Cambodia and into Thailand, Laos, and Vietnam. Rulers built regional capitals and ordered the construction of roads to connect these cities. The roads facilitated trade within the empire and also with faraway countries, such as India and China. Along the roads, King Jayavarman VII had workers build more than 100 hospitals and more than 100 traveler rest stops. Useful as the roads were to the Khmer, in 1431 they also provided a route for Thai armies to use in invading and capturing the city of Angkor.

Reading Time _____

Recalling Facts

1. The civilization of the ancient Khmer can be divided into
   - ❏ a. three periods.
   - ❏ b. temples and cities.
   - ❏ c. two geographic areas.

2. In 802 Jayavarman II proclaimed himself ruler of Cambodia and
   - ❏ a. built hospitals and rest stops.
   - ❏ b. built roads to connect cities in the empire.
   - ❏ c. identified himself with the Hindu god Shiva.

3. Rulers ordered the construction of reservoirs and canals to provide
   - ❏ a. barriers against invaders.
   - ❏ b. places for people to fish.
   - ❏ c. water during the dry season.

4. The Khmer empire attained its greatest size during the
   - ❏ a. Angkor period.
   - ❏ b. pre-Angkor period.
   - ❏ c. post-Angkor period.

5. Rulers ordered the construction of roads to
   - ❏ a. connect the capital cities of the empire.
   - ❏ b. provide a route for Thai armies.
   - ❏ c. make it easy to get to the hospitals.

Understanding Ideas

6. One can conclude from the passage that the Angkor period ended when
   - ❏ a. the irrigation systems failed.
   - ❏ b. Thai armies captured Angkor.
   - ❏ c. Jayavarman II proclaimed himself the ruler of Cambodia.

7. It is likely that one of the most important foods during the Khmer civilization was
   - ❏ a. beef.
   - ❏ b. rice.
   - ❏ c. crocodile meat.

8. One can conclude from the passage that, during the Angkor period, cities were
   - ❏ a. busy, crowded places.
   - ❏ b. reserved for royalty only.
   - ❏ c. scarce and widely separated.

9. One can conclude that, during the post-Angkor period, the Khmer civilization was
   - ❏ a. involved in sea trade.
   - ❏ b. exposed to Christianity.
   - ❏ c. influenced by Thai culture.

10. One can infer from the passage that Jayavarman VII was
    - ❏ a. worried only about expanding his empire.
    - ❏ b. concerned with the welfare of his subjects.
    - ❏ c. interested mainly in building beautiful temples.

Touring Ancient Khmer Ruins

Linda thought about the ruins she had toured at Angkor Archaeological Park in Cambodia, which contained the remains of many Khmer capitals from the 800s to the 1400s. She had started with the elaborately ornamented Angkor Wat, built as a Hindu temple in the 1100s. During her visit, she learned that Khmer temples are symbolic replicas of the Hindu universe. To reach the five decorated towers at the center of Angkor Wat, she crossed a moat, which signify the oceans surrounding the universe. Next, she passed through a series of covered passages—called galleries—that symbolize the mountain chains that encircled the center of the universe. Then she arrived at the five towers, which represent Mount Meru, the center of the universe, where the gods resided.

Over the next two days, she toured the remains of Angkor Thom, a capital city constructed in about 1200. The Bayon Temple stood at its center. More than 50 stone towers adorned the temple, each with four colossal faces carved upon it. The towers contrasted completely with those of Angkor Wat, and the carvings decorating Bayon also have different themes. They show historic events and the everyday life of the Khmer.

Now Linda was going to visit Khmer ruins in Phimai, Thailand, formerly a trade center linked by road to Angkor.

1. **Recognizing Words in Context**

   Find the word *replicas* in the passage. One definition below is closest to the meaning of that word. One definition has the opposite or nearly the opposite meaning. The remaining definition has a completely different meaning. Label the definitions C for *closest*, O for *opposite or nearly opposite,* and D for *different.*

   _____ a. originals

   _____ b. copies

   _____ c. reptiles

2. **Distinguishing Fact from Opinion**

   Two of the statements below present *facts,* which can be proved. The other statement is an *opinion,* which expresses someone's thoughts or beliefs. Label the statements F for *fact* and O for *opinion.*

   _____ a. The remains of many Khmer capitals are in Angkor Archaeological Park.

   _____ b. The faces on the towers at Bayon are awe inspiring.

   _____ c. The carvings in Bayon Temple show the everyday life of the Khmer.

3. Keeping Events in Order

Number the statements below 1, 2, and 3 to show the order in which the events took place.

_____ a. Linda passed through galleries.

_____ b. To reach the center of Angkor Wat, Linda crossed a moat.

_____ c. Linda arrived at the five towers.

4. Making Correct Inferences

Two of the statements below are correct *inferences,* or reasonable guesses. They are based on information in the passage. The other statement is an incorrect, or faulty, inference. Label the statements C for *correct* inference and F for *faulty* inference.

_____ a. Angkor Archaeological Park covers a large area.

_____ b. The Bayon Temple represents Mount Meru.

_____ c. The carvings at Angkor Wat show scenes of daily life.

5. Understanding Main Ideas

One of the statements below expresses the main idea of the passage. One statement is too general, or too broad. The other explains only part of the passage; it is too narrow. Label the statements M for *main idea,* B for *too broad,* and N for *too narrow.*

_____ a. Angkor Wat is an elaborately decorated Khmer ruin that was built as a Hindu temple in the 1100s.

_____ b. Khmer ruins, including temples and capital cities, reveal religious beliefs and historical information.

_____ c. Ancient ruins can be found in Cambodia and Thailand.

Correct Answers, Part A _____

Correct Answers, Part B _____

Total Correct Answers _____

Is there a limit to the number of years that a person can expect to live? Can changes in lifestyle add years to one's life? Throughout history people have sought answers to these questions and others.

Various myths offer the hope of great longevity. In the imaginary land of Shangri-La, for example, people are said to lead a charmed existence for a thousand years. The Spanish explorer Ponce de Leon was convinced that he would find the Fountain of Youth in what is now the state of Florida. According to the Bible, Methuselah lived to be more than 900 years old.

The subject of longevity is fascinating, and scientists study individuals such as Jeanne Calment to learn about the aging process. Calment died in 1997 in Arles, France, at the age of 122. She never married, and she lived in her own apartment until moving to a retirement community when she was 109.

Most scientists agree that bodies will last, at best, about 125 years. This potential has changed little since modern human beings appeared more than 100 thousand years ago. Recent improvements in medicine and the environment have extended life expectancy, especially for those from poorer parts of the world. It is not clear, however, whether such improvements will lengthen life expectancy beyond a certain point.

Life expectancy is the number of years an infant can be expected to live, given the conditions into which it is born. Life expectancy, therefore, is affected by nutrition, medical care, and social and political circumstances. An individual's genetic makeup is also an important factor. Children from long-lived families can hope to enjoy long lives themselves. According to recent data, the average life expectancy worldwide in 1998 was 67 years. This can be compared with an average life expectancy of 77 in the United States.

In 1970 the average life expectancy worldwide was 61 years, or 6 years less than it was in 1998. This same period saw a drop in infant mortality—the death of a child before the first birthday—from 80 births out of 1,000 to 54 births out of 1,000. According to some researchers, the rise in the average life expectancy is due primarily to the drop in infant mortality. It is not so much that adults are living to an older age. It is, rather, that more people are living into adulthood because more children are surviving beyond their first birthdays.

Reading Time _____

Recalling Facts

1. Most scientists agree that human bodies can last about
   - ❑ a. 77 years.
   - ❑ b. 100 years.
   - ❑ c. 125 years.

2. Life expectancy is the
   - ❑ a. age of a person at the time of death.
   - ❑ b. number of years an infant can be expected to live.
   - ❑ c. quality of life offered in a particular environment.

3. Infant mortality is defined as
   - ❑ a. the number of children born alive.
   - ❑ b. the kinds of behavior typical of very young children.
   - ❑ c. the number of children, out of 1,000 births, who die before their first birthday.

4. Improvements in medicine and the environment
   - ❑ a. will extend life expectancy indefinitely.
   - ❑ b. are most helpful in wealthier parts of the world.
   - ❑ c. have extended life expectancy.

5. Jeanne Calment
   - ❑ a. died in 1997 at the age of 122.
   - ❑ b. lived in France and died at the age of 109.
   - ❑ c. lived to be very old because she never married.

Understanding Ideas

6. Although it may be possible to improve the life expectancy of a particular group of people,
   - ❑ a. it is more difficult to affect the rate of infant mortality.
   - ❑ b. it is unlikely that one will be able to extend the potential life span of human beings in general.
   - ❑ c. the process of evolution is extending the potential life span beyond 125 years.

7. It is probable that scientists study long-lived people such as Calment to
   - ❑ a. improve the lives of the elderly.
   - ❑ b. identify causes of longevity.
   - ❑ c. test new therapies that might further extend life.

8. One can infer that people have at times imagined that
   - ❑ a. people live longer in the state of Florida.
   - ❑ b. a long life is a burden rather than a blessing.
   - ❑ c. it is possible to find a way to live for centuries.

9. When a person such as Calment lives a very long time, it is most likely that
   - ❑ a. he or she belonged to a very large family.
   - ❑ b. his or her family members lived to an advanced age.
   - ❑ c. there were no wars or other global disturbances taking place.

10. One can conclude that
   - ❑ a. the aging process can be arrested.
   - ❑ b. the aging process is inevitable.
   - ❑ c. life expectancy in the United States will soon reach 125 years.

The Growth of Gray Power

The segment of the American population called the baby-boom generation consists of people born between 1946 and 1964. The eldest members of this generation will soon retire. Thanks to a lifetime of good nutrition and health care, most can expect to live to the age of 77. When the youngest members turn 65, boomers will make up about 20 percent of the total population.

These numbers will avail many children of the opportunity to know their grandparents. The accumulated expertise and wisdom of those lifetimes will also be there longer than in the past for the good of society in general.

Furthermore, the rise in the number of senior citizens may affect the way the U.S. government sets its priorities. Statistics show that more older people vote than younger people. In 1996, for instance, fewer than half the registered voters between the ages of 25 and 44 voted, casting 39 percent of the ballots. About two-thirds of registered voters aged 45 and older voted. They cast 53 percent of the ballots, demonstrating what is sometimes called "gray power."

Politicians tend to focus their campaigns on people most likely to go to the polls. Once in office, they support legislation that is popular with those who elected them. This suggests that gray may very well become the color of political power.

1. **Recognizing Words in Context**

   Find the word *avail* in the passage. One definition below is closest to the meaning of that word. One definition has the opposite or nearly the opposite meaning. The remaining definition has a completely different meaning. Label the definitions C for *closest*, O for *opposite or nearly opposite*, and D for *different*.

   _____ a. benefit

   _____ b. hinder

   _____ c. entice

2. **Distinguishing Fact from Opinion**

   Two of the statements below present *facts*, which can be proved. The other statement is an *opinion*, which expresses someone's thoughts or beliefs. Label the statements F for *fact* and O for *opinion*.

   _____ a. Baby boomers are of the generation born between 1946 and 1964.

   _____ b. Statistics show that older people vote in greater numbers than younger ones.

   _____ c. Older people have more wisdom than younger people.

3. Keeping Events in Order

Number the statements below 1, 2, and 3 to show the order in which the events took place.

_____ a. The baby boom gets underway.

_____ b. In the 1996 election, people 45 and older cast 53 percent of the ballots.

_____ c. Baby boomers make up 20 percent of the population.

4. Making Correct Inferences

Two of the statements below are correct *inferences*, or reasonable guesses. They are based on information in the passage. The other statement is an incorrect, or faulty, inference. Label the statements C for *correct* inference and F for *faulty* inference.

_____ a. Senior citizens make important contributions to society.

_____ b. The baby-boom generation is larger than those that came just before and just after it.

_____ c. Young people are not as conscientious as seniors.

5. Understanding Main Ideas

One of the statements below expresses the main idea of the passage. One statement is too general, or too broad. The other explains only part of the passage; it is too narrow. Label the statements M for *main idea*, B for *too broad*, and N for *too narrow*.

_____ a. Members of the baby-boom generation are likely to hold a great deal of political power as senior citizens.

_____ b. The demographics of political power are changing in the United States.

_____ c. Thanks to a lifetime of good nutrition and health care, the average life expectancy of baby boomers is 77.

Correct Answers, Part A _____

Correct Answers, Part B _____

Total Correct Answers _____

The Stock Market: Its Bulls and Bears

The stock market is an organized marketplace in which one can buy and sell stocks and bonds. It is regulated by the Securities and Exchange Commission (SEC), an agency of the U.S. government.

People purchase shares of stock in a company, expecting to receive regular payments called dividends. Dividends represent a percentage of the company's profits. Apart from this income, the shares themselves can benefit the investor as they increase in value and, when sold, produce a capital gain.

Bonds are another kind of investment in the stock market. Whereas a share of stock represents ownership in a company, a bond represents a loan. Investments in the form of bonds are actually loans for which the company agrees to pay a set rate of interest. At the end of a specified period, the money must be repaid, along with any interest that has accrued.

There is always the risk, however, that an investment in the stock market will be money wasted. Every purchase is a gamble. Even the most reputable company can experience a bad business year and see its share price decline and its dividend income fall.

Over an extended period, a rising stock market is called a bull market and a falling one a bear market. Although short-term fluctuations are insignificant and most people take little notice of occasional dips in their investments, a sustained trend is another matter. Most people agree that a 20 percent change in the market is evidence that the bulls or the bears have gained the upper hand.

When the market is bullish, it is comparatively easy for investors to make money, and rosy economic times fuel investor enthusiasm. When the market is falling, however, cleverness and experience are required to understand when to buy stock and when to sell. Bear markets are often a feature of downturns in the economy, and it is not unusual for those who have just invested enormous sums in the market to see most of their money disappear.

The origin of these terms is mysterious. *Bear* may refer to "bearskin jobbers" who worked in the fur trade some 200 years ago. The expressions may also compare the markets to combat technique. A bull thrusts its horns upward into its opponent and a bear swipes downward with its paws. The idea of a contest between bulls and bears dates back to the Middle Ages, when animal fights were popular entertainment.

Reading Time _____

Recalling Facts

1. The Securities and Exchange Commission, which regulates the stock market,
   - ❑ a. is a private business.
   - ❑ b. is an agency of the U.S. government.
   - ❑ c. invented the terms *bull* and *bear* to describe market movements.

2. Shares of stock can provide income
   - ❑ a. only in times of a bear market.
   - ❑ b. through regular payments called dividends.
   - ❑ c. at the end of the period, when the loan must be repaid.

3. Bonds are
   - ❑ a. not a means of investing in the stock market.
   - ❑ b. short-term fluctuations representing a 20 percent change in the market.
   - ❑ c. loans for which a company agrees to pay an investor a set rate of interest.

4. When the market is bullish,
   - ❑ a. investors prefer to buy bonds.
   - ❑ b. the stock market is falling in value.
   - ❑ c. it is comparatively easy for investors to make money.

5. Bear markets are often a feature of
   - ❑ a. good economic times.
   - ❑ b. downturns in the economy.
   - ❑ c. short-term fluctuations in the value of investments.

Understanding Ideas

6. Investing in the stock market is a form of gambling because
   - ❑ a. a reputable company will always earn money.
   - ❑ b. there is no guarantee that an investment will earn money.
   - ❑ c. the market is regulated by an agency of the U.S. government.

7. A bull or a bear market is
   - ❑ a. likely to last months or even years.
   - ❑ b. an unusual situation for most investors.
   - ❑ c. easily predicted by people familiar with investing.

8. One can infer that fluctuations are
   - ❑ a. brief and repeated changes.
   - ❑ b. a sustained trend lasting several years.
   - ❑ c. references to fights between bulls and bears.

9. A person who buys a stock at a low price and expects it to rise in value is best described as a
   - ❑ a. bull.
   - ❑ b. bear.
   - ❑ c. bond trader.

10. Which of the following statements is likely to be false?
    - ❑ a. Stocks can go down in value for brief periods and still earn money for an investor.
    - ❑ b. Investing in stocks during a bull market will ensure good earnings for an investor.
    - ❑ c. Selling shares of stock for less than was paid for them will cause the investor to lose money.

Trading on the NASDAQ

NASDAQ, the National Association of Securities Dealers Automatic Quotation system, is an over-the-counter (OTC) market in which business is conducted almost entirely online. An OTC market is different from a stock exchange. In a stock exchange, dealers work face to face in one location. An OTC market can often respond more quickly to an investor's needs. This speed, however, can lead to abrupt changes in the value of stocks.

Activity on the NASDAQ is tracked at the MarketSite Tower located in Times Square in New York City. The tower supports a screen that is seven stories high and provides market news 24 hours a day.

Companies that sell shares of stock usually belong either to a stock exchange or an OTC market. NASDAQ is the largest and most popular of the OTC markets, listing more than 4,000 businesses, many of which focus on high technology. In 1999, it became the largest stock market in the United States in terms of the dollar value of its trades.

The strength of a stock market is shown by a number called a composite index. Several ratings are merged to get this number. NASDAQ began in 1971 with a base composite index of 100. The index went to more than 5,000 in 2000 and stood at 1348.31 at the end of 2002.

1. **Recognizing Words in Context**

   Find the word *composite* in the passage. One definition below is closest to the meaning of that word. One definition has the opposite or nearly the opposite meaning. The remaining definition has a completely different meaning. Label the definitions C for *closest*, O for *opposite or nearly opposite*, and D for *different*.

   _____ a. blended

   _____ b. internal

   _____ c. single

2. **Distinguishing Fact from Opinion**

   Two of the statements below present *facts*, which can be proved. The other statement is an *opinion*, which expresses someone's thoughts or beliefs. Label the statements F for *fact* and O for *opinion*.

   _____ a. An OTC's speed of response makes it a more favorable market for investors.

   _____ b. Business in an OTC market is conducted almost entirely online.

   _____ c. NASDAQ provides market news 24 hours a day at its MarketSite Tower.

3. Keeping Events in Order

Number the statements below 1, 2, and 3 to show the order in which the events took place.

_____ a. NASDAQ becomes the largest U.S. stock market in terms of the dollar value of its trades.

_____ b. NASDAQ establishes a base composite index of 100.

_____ c. NASDAQ ends the year with a composite index of 1348.31.

4. Making Correct Inferences

Two of the statements below are correct *inferences,* or reasonable guesses. They are based on information in the passage. The other statement is an incorrect, or faulty, inference. Label the statements C for *correct* inference and F for *faulty* inference.

_____ a. NASDAQ has suffered huge losses since achieving its high point in 2000.

_____ b. Online OTC markets will soon replace face-to-face stock exchanges.

_____ c. Investors with an interest in high technology companies pay particular attention to NASDAQ.

5. Understanding Main Ideas

One of the statements below expresses the main idea of the passage. One statement is too general, or too broad. The other explains only part of the passage; it is too narrow. Label the statements M for *main idea*, B for *too broad*, and N for *too narrow.*

_____ a. The stock market provides a way for individuals to invest in a variety of businesses.

_____ b. NASDAQ is a U.S. stock market that conducts its business mainly over the Internet.

_____ c. NASDAQ's MarketSite Tower is located in Times Square in New York City.

Correct Answers, Part A _____

Correct Answers, Part B _____

Total Correct Answers _____

The Coldest Continent

Antarctica is the coldest, driest, and windiest continent in the world. Located at the southernmost point of the earth, Antarctica covers and surrounds the South Pole. Scientists have recorded temperatures below –128° F. Blizzards batter the continent, and katabatic—or gravity-driven—winds blow toward its coast from the higher elevations in its interior.

Most of Antarctica is covered by ice, some of it nearly three miles thick. This icecap is made of compressed layers of snow and ice that have collected for millions of years. It shrouds mountains, valleys, lakes, and other geographic features.

Antarctica is not the smallest of the seven continents because of its thick layer of ice. In fact, it is larger than both Australia and Europe. Its tremendous polar icecap is constantly moving and reshaping the continent, forming valleys and mountains, and extending Antarctica's borders as masses of ice glide slowly downhill toward the coast and into the ocean. When these ice masses reach the ocean, chunks of ice occasionally break off, forming floating islands called icebergs. The Antarctic icecap contains about 70 percent of Earth's freshwater. Scientists estimate that if it melted, ocean levels would rise dramatically and submerge coastal cities around the world.

Despite the quantity of freshwater locked in its icecap, Antarctica is actually a desert. Its interior receives an average of about two inches of precipitation each year. Nonetheless, algae thrive on the polar ice that carpets Antarctica and the plentiful icebergs that surround the continent. Mosses and lichens cling to some of Antarctica's rocks. Despite the extreme cold, midges, lice, mites, and ticks are able to survive in Antarctica. These insects and arachnids seek the heat of living things (such as mosses, seals, and birds) to keep alive.

The frigid waters surrounding Antarctica abound in marine life. This fact makes it possible for birds to live on the continent. Algae and phytoplankton, tiny marine plants, form the foundation of Antarctica's food web. Shrimplike krill feast on these organisms; and, in turn, squid, fish, seals, whales, and birds such as penguins gobble up the krill. In this environment, apparently no organism is safe from the hungry jaws of the predators. Even whales become prey to other whales. For example, the orca, or killer whale, sometimes supplements its diet of fish, squid, seals, and penguins with smaller whales. Thus, despite being a land of extremes, Antarctica supports numerous life forms.

Reading Time _____

Recalling Facts

1. Antarctica is the coldest and _____ continent.
   - ❏ a. driest
   - ❏ b. wettest
   - ❏ c. smallest

2. Scientists estimate that a melted Antarctic ice cap would
   - ❏ a. lower water levels.
   - ❏ b. submerge coastal cities.
   - ❏ c. flood all continents.

3. Antarctica is
   - ❏ a. a desert.
   - ❏ b. an iceberg.
   - ❏ c. a continent devoid of life.

4. Antarctica's food web is based on
   - ❏ a. algae and krill.
   - ❏ b. krill and phytoplankton.
   - ❏ c. algae and phytoplankton.

5. Katabatic winds blow
   - ❏ a. around icebergs.
   - ❏ b. from the interior to the coast.
   - ❏ c. across the oceans into Antarctica.

Understanding Ideas

6. One can conclude that Antarctica was
   - ❏ a. a supply stop for European explorers.
   - ❏ b. uninhabited by people until modern times.
   - ❏ c. inhabited by large numbers of people in ancient times.

7. Antarctica would probably be a good source for
   - ❏ a. meat.
   - ❏ b. lumber.
   - ❏ c. drinking water.

8. Birds can live on Antarctica because
   - ❏ a. the oceans are frigid.
   - ❏ b. marine life abounds in the water.
   - ❏ c. they are not part of the food web.

9. Extreme cold would probably kill _____ if they were denied the heat of living things.
   - ❏ a. fish
   - ❏ b. plants
   - ❏ c. insects and arachnids

10. If Antarctica's icecap melted, it is probable that Antarctica would
    - ❏ a. have more blizzards.
    - ❏ b. become even colder.
    - ❏ c. become the smallest continent.

A Bird Lover's View of Antarctica

Many ornithologists find Antarctica intriguing and dynamic. This is because it is considered one of the best places in the world to study birds, including several kinds of penguins. More than 40 species of birds congregate there during the summer season, which lasts from December through February.

Despite Antarctica's being Earth's coldest continent, its waters teem with fish, squid, and shrimplike krill that appeal to such birds as albatrosses, petrels, gulls, and terns. These birds migrate to Antarctica to feed and to lay eggs.

Amazingly, some species of penguins remain all year, despite subzero temperatures and icy blizzards. Penguins have long downy feathers beneath their short, thick, waterproof outer feathers. Below the skin are several layers of blubber that keep them warm underwater. This is important because penguins spend most of their time swimming. Some species come onto land only to lay eggs and raise young.

Penguins are captivating birds, and some have unusual habits. Adélie penguins, for instance, feed their chicks in an interesting manner. After eating, a parent returns to its chicks and forces them to chase it. Following a heated pursuit, the parent regurgitates food for the first chick that reaches it. This might sound disgusting, but it is critical to an Adélie penguin chick's survival, and survival is what counts in Antarctica.

1. **Recognizing Words in Context**

   Find the word *captivating* in the passage. One definition below is closest to the meaning of that word. One definition has the opposite or nearly the opposite meaning. The remaining definition has a completely different meaning. Label the definitions C for *closest,* O for *opposite or nearly opposite,* and D for *different.*

   _____ a. capturing

   _____ b. fascinating

   _____ c. uninteresting

2. **Distinguishing Fact from Opinion**

   Two of the statements below present *facts,* which can be proved. The other statement is an *opinion,* which expresses someone's thoughts or beliefs. Label the statements F for *fact* and O for *opinion.*

   _____ a. Some penguins stay in Antarctica all year.

   _____ b. Summer in Antarctica lasts from December through February.

   _____ c. Travel to Antarctica would be an adventure of a lifetime.

3. Keeping Events in Order

Number the statements below 1, 2, and 3 to show the order in which the events took place.

_____ a. The parent regurgitates food for the first chick that reaches the parent.

_____ b. An Adélie parent eats.

_____ c. The chick chases the parent.

4. Making Correct Inferences

Two of the statements below are correct *inferences,* or reasonable guesses. They are based on information in the passage. The other statement is an incorrect, or faulty, inference. Label the statements C for *correct* inference and F for *faulty* inference.

_____ a. Without blubber, penguins in Antarctica would freeze.

_____ b. The fastest Adélie chicks are most likely to survive.

_____ c. Penguins do not migrate.

5. Understanding Main Ideas

One of the statements below expresses the main idea of the passage. One statement is too general, or too broad. The other explains only part of the passage; it is too narrow. Label the statements M for *main idea,* B for *too broad,* and N for *too narrow.*

_____ a. Adélie penguins feed their chicks in an interesting manner.

_____ b. People engage in bird watching in all parts of the world.

_____ c. Despite its bitter climate, Antarctica is home to more than 40 species of birds.

Correct Answers, Part A _____

Correct Answers, Part B _____

Total Correct Answers _____

The Roman Empire lasted almost 500 years. At its peak, near the end of the third century A.D., it had absorbed parts of northern Africa and the Near East, along the Mediterranean Sea, and almost all of Europe.

Roman governors enforced Rome's class system and laws. Status was based on ancestry, property and wealth, citizenship, and freedom. There were two classes, each with its own divisions, and mobility through the ranks followed a rigid set of rules. At the top were aristocrats, who were people of privilege; and below them were the plebeians. Women in all classes were considered socially and biologically inferior to men. Women could not vote, hold public office, or choose a mate, but they could own and inherit property.

The aristocrats included the patricians who were rich landowners. Senators, an elite group of 600 men from this class, also held the highest offices and judgeships in the empire. Senators could expect to move up through several ranks, of which consul was the highest. Below patricians were equestrians. These were businessmen working in financial realms— such as banking and tax collection, commerce, and public building projects.

Plebeians were citizens employed as teachers, doctors, actors, musicians, craftsmen, and manual laborers. Some were peasants, subsisting on what they could force from the soil. Many were unemployed. They were power-less in general, but most emperors made a point of controlling food prices and offering free entertainment to keep them happy—or at least quiet.

At the bottom of the social ladder were freedmen, slaves, and various noncitizens. Slaves were crucial to the empire's economy and at one point made up about 40 percent of the population. Although many of them were treated harshly, even cruelly, others were valued for their skills and knowledge. Slaves were not necessarily doomed to a lifetime of slavery. They could buy their own freedom or be freed by their owners in a process called "manumission." Formal manumission as handled by a magistrate gave the freed slave full Roman citizenship.

Money and achievement, however, began to rival ancestry as a way to move up in life. The culture and wealth of the provinces made themselves felt in the capital city of Rome. Citizenship was extended to conquered peoples—and later, provincials were admitted to the Senate. Social change was felt at the highest levels when in A.D. 193 Publius Helvius Pertinax, a freedman's son, became emperor.

Reading Time _____

Recalling Facts

1. In the Roman Empire, members of the patrician class
   - ❏ a. were people of privilege.
   - ❏ b. included slaves and freemen.
   - ❏ c. hoped to become aristocrats.

2. The group of patricians holding the highest offices and judgeships were the
   - ❏ a. senators.
   - ❏ b. equestrians.
   - ❏ c. magistrates.

3. Plebeians were Roman citizens who
   - ❏ a. entertained the patricians.
   - ❏ b. lived in the distant provinces.
   - ❏ c. were employed in various professions and as craftsmen or manual laborers.

4. At one point, about 40 percent of the empire's population consisted of
   - ❏ a. slaves.
   - ❏ b. plebeians.
   - ❏ c. freedmen.

5. Manumission is
   - ❏ a. a form of handicrafts.
   - ❏ b. the name for a lifetime of slavery.
   - ❏ c. the process through which slaves could gain their freedom.

Understanding Ideas

6. One can infer that the smallest social class in the Roman Empire was
   - ❏ a. the patrician class.
   - ❏ b. the aristocratic class.
   - ❏ c. the people living in the provinces.

7. The word *provincial* is probably used to describe people
   - ❏ a. who live in the center of a culture.
   - ❏ b. who are wealthy and powerful.
   - ❏ c. living at a distance from the center of a culture.

8. Once can conclude that, in the later years of the empire,
   - ❏ a. social status became less important.
   - ❏ b. slave labor became more important to the economy.
   - ❏ c. it became somewhat easier to improve one's social status.

9. A synonym for the adjective *plebian* might be
   - ❏ a. common.
   - ❏ b. specialized.
   - ❏ c. aristocratic.

10. One can infer that a man who had undergone formal manumission
    - ❏ a. had the same rights as an equestrian.
    - ❏ b. had more rights than a patrician woman.
    - ❏ c. could then regard himself as a member of the patrician class.

11 | B — Helena: From Tavern Girl to Empress to Saint

Flavia Julia Helena most likely came from Illyricum, in Eastern Europe, or Bithynia, in modern Turkey. Born in the middle years of the third century, she apparently worked as a tavern girl. While still in her teens, she met an ambitious soldier, Constantius, whom she may or may not have married. They had a son, Constantine, in 274.

Constantius left Helena to wed the stepdaughter of the emperor. There is no record of where Helena went or what she did. When Constantine succeeded Constantius as emperor, he brought Helena to live with him.

Constantine converted to Christianity and imposed the new religion on the formerly pagan empire. He seems to have persuaded Helena to convert as well. She became his most successful ambassador and missionary. When she was in her seventies, she traveled throughout Palestine and the East. According to legend, she was present when the cross on which Jesus had been crucified was discovered in Jerusalem. For this reason and because of the churches she founded and her many acts of charity, Helena is venerated as a saint.

Helena died in about 330. Initially laid to rest in Rome, her remains were later moved to Constantinople and finally, in the ninth century, to France.

1. **Recognizing Words in Context**

   Find the word *venerated* in the passage. One definition below is closest to the meaning of that word. One definition has the opposite or nearly the opposite meaning. The remaining definition has a completely different meaning. Label the definitions C for *closest*, O for *opposite or nearly opposite*, and D for *different*.

   _____ a. ridiculed

   _____ b. unappreciated

   _____ c. honored

2. **Distinguishing Fact from Opinion**

   Two of the statements below present *facts*, which can be proved. The other statement is an *opinion*, which expresses someone's thoughts or beliefs. Label the statements F for *fact* and O for *opinion*.

   _____ a. Helena was the mother of the emperor Constantine.

   _____ b. Helena was a saintly woman.

   _____ c. Helena founded churches and performed many acts of charity.

3. Keeping Events in Order

Number the statements below 1, 2, and 3 to show the order in which the events took place.

_____ a. Constantine converted to Christianity.

_____ b. Helena traveled to Palestine and Jerusalem.

_____ c. Helena converted to Christianity.

4. Making Correct Inferences

Two of the statements below are correct *inferences,* or reasonable guesses. They are based on information in the passage. The other statement is an incorrect, or faulty, inference. Label the statements C for *correct* inference and F for *faulty* inference.

_____ a. Constantius had no concern for either Helena or Constantine.

_____ b. Helena lived to a very advanced age.

_____ c. Constantius used marriage to advance his career.

5. Understanding Main Ideas

One of the statements below expresses the main idea of the passage. One statement is too general, or too broad. The other explains only part of the passage; it is too narrow. Label the statements M for *main idea,* B for *too broad,* and N for *too narrow.*

_____ a. Helena, mother of Constantine, was a remarkable woman.

_____ b. While in her teens, Helena met the Roman soldier Constantius, with whom she had a son, Constantine, in 274.

_____ c. Helena, born in the Roman Empire in the third century, rose from humble beginnings as a tavern girl to become both mother of the emperor and a Christian saint.

Correct Answers, Part A _____

Correct Answers, Part B _____

Total Correct Answers _____

12 A Maroon Cultures

Resistance to slavery in the Americas began with escaped slaves known as Maroons. Their name came from the Spanish word *cimarrón,* which means "fugitive" or "wild one." Maroons lived in remote, wild areas to avoid being recaptured by planters or mine owners. However, they did not live in isolation. They banded together in groups of between ten and thousands.

Many Maroon settlements were wiped out by colonists, who saw the Maroons' freedom as a threat. Semi-independent Maroon communities still survive in the Caribbean, South America, Mexico, and the American Southwest. Their stories, songs, and customs preserve their heritage, blending elements from different cultures.

The process of cross-fertilization between cultures is called creolization. Brought from many parts of Africa, the Maroons had different customs and languages. They also had to learn to survive in a new land. As a result, they did not re-create the social structures they had known in Africa. Maroon cultures reflect their African roots, but they also include words, tools, and customs adopted from Native Americans and Europeans.

For example, the language spoken by the Maroons of Jamaica combines African dialects, Spanish, and English. Most of these Maroons first came from West Africa. Slavers brought them to work in the sugarcane fields after Spain conquered the island in 1509. When the English captured Jamaica in 1655, many of the Spanish settlers fled. About fifteen hundred enslaved Africans seized their chance for freedom. They escaped to the mountains and formed communities.

Plantation owners were unable to subdue the Maroons. Maroon leaders, such as Captain Cudjoe, built fortified settlements in remote mountain regions. They also used guerilla tactics, such as disguising men as trees, to harass soldiers sent to recapture them. In 1738 the British signed a peace treaty with Cudjoe's people, which allowed them to preserve their freedom.

Cudjoe's sister, known as Granny Nanny, led a large community of Maroons. According to legend, she became discouraged after the British destroyed Nanny Town. After praying for guidance, she felt led to plant some pumpkin seeds that she carried in her pocket. Soon the hill by her new refuge was covered with flourishing pumpkin vines. Nanny inspired the Maroons to continue their struggle for freedom. Today she is recognized as one of the seven national heroes of Jamaica.

Reading Time _____

Recalling Facts

1. The ancestors of today's Maroons
   - ❑ a. were colonists from Spain.
   - ❑ b. left Africa to find new trade routes.
   - ❑ c. escaped from slavery in the Americas.

2. Maroon cultures were formed by a process called
   - ❑ a. creolization.
   - ❑ b. immigration.
   - ❑ c. pacification.

3. Many Maroon customs first began in
   - ❑ a. Africa.
   - ❑ b. Indonesia.
   - ❑ c. Australia.

4. In Jamaica many Maroons escaped when
   - ❑ a. the British took over the island.
   - ❑ b. the Spanish first settled the island.
   - ❑ c. Captain Cudjoe organized a revolt.

5. In Jamaica today, Granny Nanny is remembered as a
   - ❑ a. traditional storyteller.
   - ❑ b. heroic freedom fighter.
   - ❑ c. beautiful African princess.

Understanding Ideas

6. One can conclude that the Maroons
   - ❑ a. resisted influence by European cultures.
   - ❑ b. carefully re-created their African traditions.
   - ❑ c. demonstrated courage, determination, and creativity.

7. It is likely that plantation owners tried to recapture the Jamaican Maroons because they
   - ❑ a. thought that the Maroons were poor fighters.
   - ❑ b. feared that other captive Africans would escape to join them.
   - ❑ c. wanted to keep the Maroons from making an alliance with the British.

8. Compared with the British soldiers sent to capture them, the Jamaican Maroons
   - ❑ a. had poor discipline.
   - ❑ b. had better equipment.
   - ❑ c. were better at guerilla warfare.

9. One sign that the planters respected the power of the Jamaican Maroons is the
   - ❑ a. name Maroon.
   - ❑ b. destruction of Nanny Town.
   - ❑ c. treaty signed with Captain Cudjoe.

10. Historians believe that the Maroons are important because the group shows how
    - ❑ a. African captives resisted slavery.
    - ❑ b. traditional cultures resist adaptation.
    - ❑ c. Native Americans learned to fortify their towns.

Tales of Ti Malice

Historians are still learning about ways that captive Africans resisted slavery. Those who defied their masters or ran away faced severe punishment. As a result, enslaved people sought other ways to outwit their captors. Stories brought from Africa about the trickster Ti Malice allegorize, or express imaginatively, ways that those who seem powerless can thwart the powerful.

Some folklorists say that Ti Malice was originally Anansi, the popular African spider trickster. In Caribbean tales, Anansi becomes two characters: Ti Malice and his victim, Uncle Bouki. Ti Malice is a clever, sometimes ruthless, practical joker. Uncle Bouki is a stubborn peasant who thinks that he is smarter than he is.

In one story, Uncle Bouki observes an old man relishing his dinner. As the man bites into a hot pepper, he exclaims, "Whee-ai!" Bouki asks where he may find some of that delectable whee-ai. Seizing the opportunity, Ti Malice prepares a sack with oranges and pineapples on the top and cactus leaves concealed on the bottom. When he invites Bouki to reach in, his gullible victim grabs the cactus leaves and cries, "Whee-ai!"

Another story in the Malice-Bouki cycle became popular in the United States as the tale of Br'er Rabbit and the Tar Baby. These tales are still told for entertainment. Behind the jokes, however, lies another story: resistance to captivity.

1. Recognizing Words in Context

Find the word *allegorize* in the passage. One definition below is closest to the meaning of that word. One definition has the opposite or nearly the opposite meaning. The remaining definition has a completely different meaning. Label the definitions C for *closest,* O for *opposite or nearly opposite,* and D for *different.*

_____ a. illustrate

_____ b. conceal

_____ c. seize

2. Distinguishing Fact from Opinion

Two of the statements below present *facts,* which can be proved. The other statement is an *opinion,* which expresses someone's thoughts or beliefs. Label the statements F for *fact* and O for *opinion.*

_____ a. Many stories have been told about Ti Malice.

_____ b. Ti Malice usually gets the best of Uncle Bouki.

_____ c. Stories about Ti Malice are funnier than stories about Br'er Rabbit.

3. Keeping Events in Order

Number the statements below 1, 2, and 3 to show the order in which the events took place.

_____ a. People enslaved in Jamaica told stories about African tricksters.

_____ b. Anansi stories were told in Africa.

_____ c. Storytellers developed many stories about Ti Malice and Uncle Bouki.

4. Making Correct Inferences

Two of the statements below are correct *inferences*, or reasonable guesses. They are based on information in the passage. The other statement is an incorrect, or faulty, inference. Label the statements C for *correct* inference and F for *faulty* inference.

_____ a. Captives brought from Africa handed down stories about the trickster Anansi.

_____ b. Plantation owners made up stories about Ti Malice to deceive enslaved Africans.

_____ c. Trickster stories are popular in many countries.

5. Understanding Main Ideas

One of the statements below expresses the main idea of the passage. One statement is too general, or too broad. The other explains only part of the passage; it is too narrow. Label the statements M for *main idea*, B for *too broad*, and N for *too narrow*.

_____ a. Ti Malice tricked Uncle Bouki into grabbing some cactus leaves.

_____ b. People who study folklore have found common elements in trickster tales.

_____ c. Stories about Ti Malice showed captives ways they could resist their masters.

Correct Answers, Part A _____

Correct Answers, Part B _____

Total Correct Answers _____

Throughout time, people have worn shoes and other footwear for a variety of reasons, including protection, fashion, and status. Scientists and historians do not know when the shoe was invented. However, they do know that people have been wearing shoes for thousands of years. As early as 3700 B.C., the ancient Egyptians wore sandals, possibly to protect their feet from rocks and hot desert sands. In very cold climates, people wore furry baglike foot coverings or boots to keep their feet from freezing. Much later, European knights wore armor as protection from their enemies' weapons; and at various times in history, ladies in Europe and Asia have worn elevated shoes to keep their feet clean and dry. Women have also worn pedestal shoes to give themselves an appearance of height and elegance.

Historians have documented how footwear changed through history, proving that changing fashions are not limited to the present. In some cases, contact between different cultures caused styles to change. For example, by trading with Europeans, Native Americans acquired beads. They used these to decorate moccasins and other clothing. Marco Polo brought the platform shoe from China to Venice, where it became popular.

Seemingly frivolous shoe styles became popular at various times in history. About the 1300s, men's shoes with long, pointed toes were fashionable in Europe. The fashion, known as the cracow, spread west from Poland, although European crusaders may have been inspired by the slippers with turned-up toes that they saw in Asia. In any event, the toes of some cracows were so long that wearers fastened a chain to the toe of each shoe and attached the chain to their knees. Following the cracow, an extremely wide-toed shoe called the duckbill, bearpaw, cowmouth, or hornbill was popular in Europe. Eventually lawmakers limited the width of the toe.

Following the popularity of wide-toed shoes, high heels became trendy. Wealthy European men and women imitated these styles, which were worn by the French royal court. Simpler, flat-heeled shoes came into style by the end of the 1700s, after French revolutionaries removed the king and his court from power. By the 1830s, square-toed shoes were again in fashion, although they were not so wide as they had been hundreds of years earlier.

Today people wear sandals, boots, high heels, flat shoes, platform shoes, and shoes with pointy, square, or round toes. Designers can look to styles of the past and recycle them today.

Reading Time _____

Recalling Facts

1. Scientists and historians do not know
   - ❑ a. when the shoe was invented.
   - ❑ b. why knights wore armor.
   - ❑ c. the width of the square-toed shoe.

2. In some cases, contact between different cultures
   - ❑ a. resulted in changing styles.
   - ❑ b. caused boots to become popular.
   - ❑ c. resulted in the outlawing of certain types of shoes.

3. A popular men's shoe with long, pointed toes, in about the 1300s, was the
   - ❑ a. sandal.
   - ❑ b. cracow.
   - ❑ c. moccasin.

4. Like the platform shoe, the cracow is an example of a
   - ❑ a. slipper.
   - ❑ b. reliable work shoe.
   - ❑ c. fashion that spread from one part of the world to another.

5. High heels became popular among wealthy Europeans who
   - ❑ a. liked cow mouths.
   - ❑ b. imitated the styles worn by the French royal court.
   - ❑ c. were influenced by the styles of the English royal family.

Understanding Ideas

6. Before people wore shoes, it is likely that they
   - ❑ a. lived in moderate climates.
   - ❑ b. could not hunt large animals.
   - ❑ c. rode horses during the winter months.

7. It is likely that a man used a chain to attach the toes of his cracows to his knees so that
   - ❑ a. he would not trip.
   - ❑ b. the toes would not get muddy.
   - ❑ c. greater attention could be drawn to the craftsmanship of his shoes.

8. The author remarks that some shoe styles seem frivolous; this probably means that
   - ❑ a. shoes are unnecessary.
   - ❑ b. some shoe styles are not utilitarian.
   - ❑ c. shoes were originally created to make people laugh.

9. According to the passage, the proverb that best captures the reason for changing fashions in footwear is
   - ❑ a. "Variety is the spice of life."
   - ❑ b. "Never put off 'til tomorrow what you can do today."
   - ❑ c. "The grass is always greener on the other side of the fence."

10. According to the passage, it is probable that future shoe fashions will
    - ❑ a. be different from anything seen before.
    - ❑ b. be less expensive than shoes are today.
    - ❑ c. look familiar to historians of fashion.

Jan Ernst Matzeliger came to the United States from South America in the 1870s. As a child, Matzeliger had a talent for repairing machinery. As an adult, he invented a device that revolutionized the shoe industry.

In the late 1870s, Matzeliger worked for a shoe manufacturer. At that time, machines cut and stitched the upper part of a shoe, but workers called hand lasters attached the uppers to the soles manually. Skilled hand lasters could produce 50 pairs of shoes in 10 hours and commanded high wages for their work. Even so, they could not assemble a shoe so quickly as machines could produce its parts.

Many people believed that no one could invent a machine to do the hand lasters' work, but Matzeliger disagreed. For years he labored to develop a lasting machine. He used his knowledge of shoemaking and his ingenuity to develop models. At first Matzeliger used remnants of wood, scrap metal, and other discarded materials to make his models. Instead of buying food, he spent his earnings to purchase better materials for his lasting machine.

Finally, Matzeliger's lasting machine was ready. In one day, it could assemble more than 10 times as many shoes as a person could and could produce shoes more cheaply. As a result, more people could afford to wear shoes.

1. **Recognizing Words in Context**

   Find the word *ingenuity* in the passage. One definition below is closest to the meaning of that word. One definition has the opposite or nearly the opposite meaning. The remaining definition has a completely different meaning. Label the definitions C for *closest,* O for *opposite or nearly opposite,* and D for *different.*

   _____ a. limitations

   _____ b. creativity

   _____ c. unoriginality

2. **Distinguishing Fact from Opinion**

   Two of the statements below present *facts,* which can be proved. The other statement is an *opinion,* which expresses someone's thoughts or beliefs. Label the statements F for *fact* and O for *opinion.*

   _____ a. Jan Ernst Matzeliger invented the most useful invention of the 1800s.

   _____ b. Matzeliger spent years perfecting his lasting machine.

   _____ c. Matzeliger's lasting machine changed the shoe industry.

3. Keeping Events in Order

Number the statements below 1, 2, and 3 to show the order in which the events took place.

_____ a. Matzeliger developed a talent for repairing machinery.

_____ b. Shoes were made increasingly faster and more cheaply.

_____ c. Matzeliger used discarded materials to make models of a lasting machine.

4. Making Correct Inferences

Two of the statements below are correct *inferences*, or reasonable guesses. They are based on information in the passage. The other statement is an incorrect, or faulty, inference. Label the statements C for *correct* inference and F for *faulty* inference.

_____ a. Matzeliger was often hungry.

_____ b. One reason shoes cost a lot of money was that hand lasters earned a high wage.

_____ c. Hand lasters were relieved when the lasting machine was invented because it made their job easier.

5. Understanding Main Ideas

One of the statements below expresses the main idea of the passage. One statement is too general, or too broad. The other explains only part of the passage; it is too narrow. Label the statements M for *main idea*, B for *too broad*, and N for *too narrow*.

_____ a. Jan Ernst Matzeliger's lasting machine mechanized the shoe industry and allowed more shoes to be produced at a lower cost.

_____ b. Jan Ernst Matzeliger spent many years inventing the lasting machine.

_____ c. Many inventors have made contributions to the modern shoe industry.

Correct Answers, Part A _____

Correct Answers, Part B _____

Total Correct Answers _____

Nativism and the Know-Nothing Party

Nativism is a belief system that puts the interests of white, native-born, often Protestant, Americans over those of immigrants. It reached its full force as a movement in the second half of the nineteenth century and still persists in some aspects of American thought.

Nativist thinking was evident early in the United States. Its earliest targets were Roman Catholics. Nativists claimed that the U.S. government needed voters who were educated, moral, and loyal. Catholics, they said, could not be good citizens because of their devotion to the Pope and the Church. Working people, worried that their jobs were at risk, had more concrete concerns. Immigrants who would work for less pay would drive wages down. They might even take jobs away from native-born Americans. The Irish who arrived during the 1840s were, in particular, victims of this attitude.

As the stream of immigrants became a flood during the 1840s, secret groups were founded to "protect" Americans from the onslaught. Among the best known of these was the Order of the Star Spangled Banner. It was founded in New York in 1849 and soon spread to other large cities. Members of such nativist groups were called Know Nothings. Rumor had it that when questioned, members were supposed to answer, "I know nothing."

Know Nothings formed the core of a political party officially called the American Party, which rose to power in the 1850s. The American Party aimed to protect the rights of native-born Americans. Members believed that only native-born citizens should be allowed to vote or hold office. They sought to limit the number of foreigners allowed to enter the country. They also fought for laws that required 21-year residency before a person could apply for citizenship. The Party fell apart, however, over the question of slavery. Members who supported slavery left and joined the Democrats. Those against the practice allied with the Republicans. By 1860 the American Party had become a minor group on the fringes of politics.

Nativism continues to thrive in the United States, however. Congress placed a 10-year halt on immigration from China in 1882 and then banned it entirely in 1902. In 1907 President Theodore Roosevelt persuaded Japan to disallow emigration of its citizens from Japan to the United States. For decades after 1900, efforts were made to restrict the flow of Jewish immigrants from Eastern Europe. More recently nativist concerns have focused on Latino and Hispanic peoples.

Reading Time _____

Recalling Facts

1. Nativism favors the interests of
   _____ over immigrants.
   ❑ a. Native Americans
   ❑ b. Americans of color
   ❑ c. white, native-born Americans

2. The first targets of nativist thinking
   were
   ❑ a. Roman Catholics.
   ❑ b. the Know Nothings.
   ❑ c. the poorest immigrants.

3. The Know-Nothing, or American,
   Party
   ❑ a. opposed nativist ideas in the
      1850s.
   ❑ b. was a name given to immigrants
      who did not speak English.
   ❑ c. began as secret groups founded
      to protect Americans from the
      onslaught of immigrants.

4. The American Party fell apart
   ❑ a. in the decades after 1900.
   ❑ b. because of pressure from the
      Roman Catholic Church.
   ❑ c. when its members disagreed
      over the question of slavery.

5. Recent nativist concerns
   ❑ a. have focused on Latino and
      Hispanic peoples.
   ❑ b. forced Congress to place a
      10-year halt on immigration
      from China.
   ❑ c. brought about the founding of
      the Order of the Star Spangled
      Banner.

Understanding Ideas

6. One can conclude that immigration
   in the nineteenth century
   ❑ a. brought mostly well-educated
      people to the United States.
   ❑ b. was regarded by many as a threat
      to the American way of life.
   ❑ c. did not concern most Americans.

7. One could argue that nativists
   ❑ a. saw themselves as patriotic.
   ❑ b. had full confidence in the U.S.
      government and its laws.
   ❑ c. had little concern about the role
      religion should play in society.

8. If the Know Nothings had succeeded
   in their aims, it is likely that
   ❑ a. the United States would be
      about the same as it is today.
   ❑ b. more Americans would speak
      languages other than English.
   ❑ c. the population would have been
      much less diverse than it is today.

9. One can conclude that immigration
   ❑ a. held back U.S. economic
      development.
   ❑ b. did not concern most Americans
      in the 1850s.
   ❑ c. was of greater concern on the
      East Coast than the West Coast.

10. Which sentence below best describes
    the main idea of the passage?
    ❑ a. The American Party had
       become a minor group on the
       fringe of politics by 1860.
    ❑ b. Nativism is but one outcome of
       prejudice in the American
       political arena.
    ❑ c. Nativism has influenced U.S.
       political movements to limit
       immigration.

14 B Sacco and Vanzetti: Guilty?

On August 23, 1927, Nicola Sacco and Bartolomeo Vanzetti died in the electric chair. They had been convicted of murdering two men and stealing money from a factory in South Braintree, Massachusetts, in 1920. The entire case was the subject of intense scrutiny and controversy.

Neither had a criminal record. The stolen money was never traced to either. Sacco argued that he was at the Italian consulate in Boston, not in South Braintree, on the day of the crimes. In 1925 a man also under a death sentence declared that his gang had done the deed. The judge was criticized for the way he conducted the trial.

It is possible that Sacco and Vanzetti were guilty only of being foreigners who held beliefs unpopular with the U.S. government. They supported anarchism, which advocates abolishment of the government. They had evaded the draft during World War I, had lied to the arresting officers, and as Italian immigrants had been the object of widespread prejudice.

The story of Sacco and Vanzetti is fascinating. Tests performed on Sacco's gun in 1961 suggest that it was the weapon used to kill the guard at the factory. In 1977, however, the governor of Massachusetts signed a proclamation describing the trial as flawed and clearing the names of Sacco and Vanzetti.

1. **Recognizing Words in Context**

   Find the word *scrutiny* in the passage. One definition below is closest to the meaning of that word. One definition has the opposite or nearly the opposite meaning. The remaining definition has a completely different meaning. Label the definitions C for *closest,* O for *opposite or nearly opposite,* and D for *different.*

   _____ a. avoidance

   _____ b. stimulation

   _____ c. inspection

2. **Distinguishing Fact from Opinion**

   Two of the statements below present *facts,* which can be proved. The other statement is an *opinion,* which expresses someone's thoughts or beliefs. Label the statements F for *fact* and O for *opinion.*

   _____ a. The case of Sacco and Vanzetti is the subject of controversy.

   _____ b. Sacco and Vanzetti believed in anarchism.

   _____ c. Sacco and Vanzetti were guilty of the crime of which they were accused.

3. Keeping Events in Order

Number the statements below 1, 2, and 3 to show the order in which the events took place.

_____ a. Tests on Sacco's gun suggest that it was the weapon used to kill the guard at the factory.

_____ b. Sacco and Vanzetti were executed in Massachusetts.

_____ c. A convicted criminal declared that his gang had committed the murders and robbery in South Braintree.

4. Making Correct Inferences

Two of the statements below are correct *inferences,* or reasonable guesses. They are based on information in the passage. The other statement is an incorrect, or faulty, inference. Label the statements C for *correct* inference and F for *faulty* inference.

_____ a. During the trial, public opinion about the guilt of Sacco and Vanzetti was divided.

_____ b. Sacco and Vanzetti had abided by all laws while residents of the United States.

_____ c. It is likely that Sacco and Vanzetti did not receive a fair trial.

5. Understanding Main Ideas

One of the statements below expresses the main idea of the passage. One statement is too general, or too broad. The other explains only part of the passage; it is too narrow. Label the statements M for *main idea,* B for *too broad,* and N for *too narrow.*

_____ a. Sacco and Vanzetti were executed for the murders of two men in Massachusetts.

_____ b. In the case of Sacco and Vanzetti, a flawed trial and public prejudice may have caused innocent men to be executed.

_____ c. Immigrants have often been the victims of prejudice in the United States.

Correct Answers, Part A _____

Correct Answers, Part B _____

Total Correct Answers _____

68

Descendents of the Inca

After the Spanish conquered the Incan empire in the 1500s, they tried to destroy Incan culture. They were unsuccessful, however. Inca traditions survive today, kept alive by descendents who live in Peru, Ecuador, Bolivia, and other present-day countries that once were part of the empire. Many Inca descendents live in highland villages. They speak Quechua, the language spoken by the early Inca, although today children learn Spanish at school.

Most villagers continue the agricultural traditions of their ancestors. Farmers use many traditional tools, such as the foot hoe or foot plow, and plant traditional crops on terraced hillsides and in carefully laid out fields. Many fields are high above sea level, so farmers plant crops that grow well at high altitudes. For example, in fields that are about 2.3 miles above sea level, farmers grow grains, such as quinoa and barley, and many kinds of potatoes, including sweet potatoes. At lower altitudes, people grow corn, lettuce, tomatoes, and other fruits and vegetables.

Villagers also graze herds of llamas, alpacas, and sheep. The Inca eat the meat of these animals sparingly, because these creatures are important for their wool, which the Inca spin into yarn and then weave. In the Incan empire, women were weavers, but today both boys and girls learn how to spin and weave so that they can preserve the Incan weaving tradition. They use traditional tools, such as the backstrap loom, and weave ancestral designs. Many continue to make and wear traditional clothes, such as hats, ponchos, and shawls.

Many families have no car. Instead of driving, they walk, sometimes along ancient Incan roads. Farmers walk to their fields, which may be an hour from home. People even take eight-hour walks to visit friends who live in different villages. Many people walk from one village to another to trade homegrown or homemade products at the weekly outdoor market. In some areas, where modern transportation remains rare or unavailable, people still use llamas to carry burdens.

The market is a place to trade, meet friends and family, and share news. Instead of using money, the ancient Inca bartered goods, and until recently many Inca living in the mountains maintained this tradition. Although many Inca still barter, young people often sell homemade items to raise money for school supplies.

Slowly, modern ways are encroaching upon the traditional Incan way of life, but people can keep their culture alive by practicing its traditions.

Reading Time _____

Recalling Facts

1. Many Inca descendents live in
   - ❏ a. Mexico.
   - ❏ b. the mountains.
   - ❏ c. highland villages.

2. Farmers use traditional tools, such as the
   - ❏ a. tractor.
   - ❏ b. foot hoe.
   - ❏ c. ox-drawn plow.

3. Villagers graze herds of
   - ❏ a. sheep, cows, and goats.
   - ❏ b. llamas, alpacas, and sheep.
   - ❏ c. llamas, cattle, and horses.

4. In the Incan empire, women were weavers, but today
   - ❏ a. no one knows how to spin and weave.
   - ❏ b. only the elderly remember how to spin and weave.
   - ❏ c. boys and girls learn how to spin and weave.

5. Cultural practices that many Inca descendants share with ancestors include
   - ❏ a. speaking Spanish, bartering, and growing potatoes.
   - ❏ b. making homemade items, wearing ponchos, and going to school.
   - ❏ c. speaking Quechua, planting traditional crops, and weaving.

Understanding Ideas

6. One can infer that older Inca descendents may speak
   - ❏ a. only Quechua.
   - ❏ b. as skilled interpreters.
   - ❏ c. predominantly Spanish.

7. One can infer that the most useful animal to the highland Inca is the
   - ❏ a. goat.
   - ❏ b. llama.
   - ❏ c. sheep.

8. It is likely that younger Inca are
   - ❏ a. as likely to barter as their elders.
   - ❏ b. less likely to barter than their elders.
   - ❏ c. more likely to barter than their elders.

9. It is likely that the Quechua language and Incan traditions have survived because
   - ❏ a. many Inca descendents live in remote mountain villages.
   - ❏ b. Inca descendents live in complete isolation.
   - ❏ c. the governments of Peru, Bolivia, and Chile have always valued the Incan way of life.

10. If Inca descendents do not practice their cultural traditions, it is likely that
    - ❏ a. modern customs will replace them.
    - ❏ b. highland villages will be abandoned.
    - ❏ c. all knowledge of the Inca will be lost.

Musical Instruments of the Andes

Long before the Spanish conquered the Incan empire, music was part of the Native American cultures of the Andes. Musicians played percussion and wind instruments, many of them different in sound or appearance from those that came from Europe.

Traditional Andean percussion instruments include drums and rattles. Woodwinds include quenas, sikus, and rondadors. The quena is a hollow tube with a mouthpiece at one end and finger holes along the tube. Traditionally made of bone, clay, stone, bamboo, or wood, most quenas today are made of bamboo or wood. The siku and rondador look much like panpipes; but a siku has two rows of pipes, and a rondador has one. To make a bamboo rondador, artisans cut cane of various sizes, arrange the bamboo pipes side-by-side in a row, and connect them with bamboo and leather.

After the Spanish conquest, Native Americans used available resources to create new instruments based on Spanish ones. One contemporary instrument is the charango. Like the Spanish guitar, the charango is a stringed instrument. Unlike the guitar, the body of the charango is often made of an armadillo shell. The charango gave musicians new sounds with which to work. Today many musicians play this and other traditional instruments, thus preserving the musical heritage of the Andes.

1. **Recognizing Words in Context**

   Find the word *contemporary* in the passage. One definition below is closest to the meaning of that word. One definition has the opposite or nearly the opposite meaning. The remaining definition has a completely different meaning. Label the definitions C for *closest*, O for *opposite or nearly opposite*, and D for *different*.

   _____ a. modern

   _____ b. ancient

   _____ c. predictable

2. **Distinguishing Fact from Opinion**

   Two of the statements below present *facts*, which can be proved. The other statement is an *opinion*, which expresses someone's thoughts or beliefs. Label the statements F for *fact* and O for *opinion*.

   _____ a. The body of a charango may be made of an armadillo shell.

   _____ b. Quenas made of wood produce a better sound than those made of bone.

   _____ c. A siku, unlike a rondador, has two rows of pipes.

3. Keeping Events in Order

Number the statements below 1, 2, and 3 to show the order in which the events took place.

_____ a. The Spanish conquer the Incan Empire.

_____ b. The guitar becomes popular.

_____ c. The Inca play the charango.

4. Making Correct Inferences

Two of the statements below are correct *inferences,* or reasonable guesses. They are based on information in the passage. The other statement is an incorrect, or faulty, inference. Label the statements C for *correct* inference and F for *faulty* inference.

_____ a. Native Americans stopped making traditional instruments after the Spanish conquest.

_____ b. A rondador can be made out of material other than bamboo.

_____ c. In the Andes, charangos were often made from armadillo shells because wood was scarce.

5. Understanding Main Ideas

One of the statements below expresses the main idea of the passage. One statement is too general, or too broad. The other explains only part of the passage; it is too narrow. Label the statements M for *main idea,* B for *too broad,* and N for *too narrow.*

_____ a. Andean instruments include percussion, wind, and Spanish-inspired string instruments.

_____ b. The quena, siku, and rondador are traditional Andean woodwind instruments.

_____ c. The musical heritage of Native American cultures of the Andes predates the Spanish conquest.

Correct Answers, Part A _____

Correct Answers, Part B _____

Total Correct Answers _____

Preschool: What Should It Do?

One often hears that children should arrive at school "ready to learn." For most children, the acquisition of reading and math skills starts in the first grade. In states where kindergarten is compulsory, it begins even earlier.

Many parents, teachers, and politicians assert that preschool is the best way to prepare children to learn. There is no real consensus, however, about how this preparation should be achieved.

For some, early childhood education relates to the development of the whole child. They think that preschool should be play that encourages exploration and discovery. Group activities teach positive social behaviors such as sharing, kindness, and patience. Time spent alone encourages independence. Learning letters and counting is important only for children who show an interest in them. Advocates of this approach stress that each child is unique and should learn at his or her own pace.

Other people cite research showing that children are ready to absorb basic academic concepts by age 3 or 4. They claim that early introduction to letters and numbers lays the foundation for later academic excellence. Since the 1980s, many people have stressed the value of preschool and point to the success of programs—such as Head Start—that target low-income children.

Is there proof that an academic curriculum in preschool will lead to academic success? Studies have not been conclusive.

In the short term, evidence suggests that middle-class children who attend preschool are ahead of their peers in math and language skills, as well as in social skills, when they enter school. However, the same studies show that the gap narrows considerably by the time children reach age 8.

Children living in poverty are a different matter. Those enrolled in programs such as Head Start seem to do better than impoverished children who do not attend a preschool. For instance, youngsters in one group enrolled in the program, tracked until the age of 21, earned higher scores on intelligence tests, were more likely to graduate from high school, and demonstrated more interest in higher education.

The idea of public preschools raises many issues. Providing Head Start for all children would be a financial burden on communities that already struggle to fund current school programs. Also, where would a sufficient number of teachers trained in early childhood development be found?

Reading Time _____

Recalling Facts

1. People who believe that early child-hood education is related to the development of the whole child
   - ❏ a. believe that each child should learn at his or her own pace.
   - ❏ b. do not believe in preschool for children in low-income families.
   - ❏ c. believe that, by the age of 3, children should be introduced to letters and numbers.

2. The reasoning behind early introduction to letters and numbers is
   - ❏ a. validated by extensive research.
   - ❏ b. that this lays the foundation for later academic success.
   - ❏ c. that this speeds up a child's natural development.

3. Studies that evaluate the effectiveness of preschool, in general, as a means to academic success
   - ❏ a. suggest that preschool most benefits middle-class children.
   - ❏ b. show that most children start school with similar language and social skills.
   - ❏ c. have failed to provide enough definitive information.

4. Head Start is
   - ❏ a. not a successful program.
   - ❏ b. a preschool program that targets low-income children.
   - ❏ c. a program that supports children all the way through high school.

5. People have believed in the value of preschool
   - ❏ a. since the 1980s.
   - ❏ b. since the 1950s.
   - ❏ c. since public schools systems were established.

Understanding Ideas

6. Advocates of the development of the whole child believe school readiness is
   - ❏ a. accomplished only in a preschool setting.
   - ❏ b. demonstration of intellectual, social, and emotional skills.
   - ❏ c. having basic skills, such as knowing letters and numbers.

7. States that mandate kindergarten are likely to set a curriculum that
   - ❏ a. includes academic skills.
   - ❏ b. exclusively teaches social skills.
   - ❏ c. allows parents to choose what their children will learn.

8. The study of a group of Head Start children suggests that the program
   - ❏ a. is poorly managed.
   - ❏ b. has achieved negative results.
   - ❏ c. is successful according to a broad range of measures.

9. One can conclude that states
   - ❏ a. follow the same guidelines for schooling.
   - ❏ b. have different requirements for schooling.
   - ❏ c. need to agree on the value of universal preschool.

10. Which of the following sentences best expresses the main idea?
    - ❏ a. Some children learn their letters and how to count in preschool.
    - ❏ b. The term *preschool* refers to programs for children too young to attend public school.
    - ❏ c. Preschool may help children get a better start in school, although there is disagreement about what it should offer.

| 16 | B | Head Start: An Even Start in School? |

Head Start began in 1965 as a summer program for preschool-age children from low-income families. Today, it prepares children for school and attends to their medical, emotional, and nutritional needs. Head Start is funded by the federal government through the Department of Health and Human Services. The centers are run locally by nonprofit organizations and school systems. Children from families whose income falls below the poverty line are eligible. When the Head Start Act was reauthorized in 1994, an Early Head Start program for infants and pregnant women was added. In 2002 almost 90 percent of children in Head Start were three or four years old. More than half were African American or Hispanic. About 13 percent dealt with physical, emotional, or mental challenges.

The preliminary findings of an ongoing study begun in 1997 suggest that Head Start children are socially and academically prepared to start school, yet some argue that Head Start has failed in its primary goal. Head Start, they say, cannot offer children from poor homes an even start with children from more affluent homes. There are too few Head Start classrooms, for one thing. More to the point, however, is the belief that whatever progress Head Start children make, more affluent families have access to resources that can ensure their children's beginning school better prepared.

1. **Recognizing Words in Context**

   Find the word *preliminary* in the passage. One definition below is closest to the meaning of that word. One definition has the opposite or nearly the opposite meaning. The remaining definition has a completely different meaning. Label the definitions C for *closest*, O for *opposite or nearly opposite*, and D for *different*.

   _____ a. paternal

   _____ b. final

   _____ c. initial

2. **Distinguishing Fact from Opinion**

   Two of the statements below present *facts*, which can be proved. The other statement is an *opinion*, which expresses someone's thoughts or beliefs. Label the statements F for *fact* and O for *opinion*.

   _____ a. Head Start is funded by the federal government.

   _____ b. Head Start centers are managed locally by nonprofit organizations and school systems.

   _____ c. Head Start guarantees children from low-income families a good start at school.

3. Keeping Events in Order

Number the statements below 1, 2, and 3 to show the order in which the events took place.

_____ a. The Head Start program was reauthorized.

_____ b. Findings suggested that Head Start children were socially and academically prepared to start school.

_____ c. Head Start offered a summer program for preschool-age children from low-income families.

4. Making Correct Inferences

Two of the statements below are correct *inferences,* or reasonable guesses. They are based on information in the passage. The other statement is an incorrect, or faulty, inference. Label the statements C for *correct* inference and F for *faulty* inference.

_____ a. Children from low-income homes often face more difficulties in school than children from more afflu-ent homes.

_____ b. Organizations such as school systems are in a position to identify children who might benefit from Head Start.

_____ c. Children who enter school ready to learn will be successful as students.

5. Understanding Main Ideas

One of the statements below expresses the main idea of the passage. One statement is too general, or too broad. The other explains only part of the passage; it is too narrow. Label the statements M for *main idea,* B for *too broad,* and N for *too narrow.*

_____ a. When the Head Start Act was reauthorized in 1994, an Early Head Start program for infants was added to it.

_____ b. Some preschools are private and others are public; the programs vary from center to center.

_____ c. Head Start provides services to low-income families that help prepare their children for the social and academic demands of school.

Correct Answers, Part A _____

Correct Answers, Part B _____

Total Correct Answers _____

The French Revolution and *A Tale of Two Cities*

Charles Dickens's novel *A Tale of Two Cities* is set in the years before and during the French Revolution (1789–1799). During its course, French revolutionaries overthrew the monarchy and established a republic of free and equal citizens.

In reading the work, one sees that Dickens distorted some details of the French Revolution. At the beginning, Dickens notes that, in 1775, France was busy spending money. This mention of France's spending touches briefly on what is perhaps the major cause of the French Revolution. Before the revolt, the government often borrowed money because it spent more than it raised in taxes. The increased spending and borrowing enraged many people, yet Dickens focused instead on the aristocracy's oppression and abuse of the working class, including peasants, as the causes of the revolution.

The Marquis, one of the book's characters, abuses and kills many people. Thus, he represents the nobles who mistreat the lower classes. One reviewer criticized this portrayal as an unfair depiction of French society in the mid-1700s. The reviewer pointed out that the government would have punished nobles who abused or murdered. Nobles may have been guilty of other evils, however, such as not feeding the starving masses after bad weather ruined crops in 1789.

Dickens's account of the storming of the Bastille fails to mention that the mob that stormed the prison was looking for ammunition to use in defense against a possible attack by the king's troops. Dickens does include some accurate details, however, such as the crowd's finding only seven prisoners and freeing them and the mob's beheading the prison administrator and impaling his head on a pike. At first, the women who knit as they watch the executions may seem to be an odd detail, but many women did in fact knit stockings for the war effort as they watched the guillotine at work.

Dickens's descriptions of the steady stream of condemned people into prison and the carts taking them to their deaths give readers some idea of the frequency with which officials arrested and executed people during the Reign of Terror, which lasted about a year. During the Terror, the government arrested about 250 thousand people, tried and guillotined about 17 thousand, and executed about 12 thousand without a trial. Those executed included people who opposed the revolution, people who offended the revolutionaries, and even some revolutionaries. About 15 percent were members of the clergy or nobility.

Reading Time _____

Recalling Facts

1. *A Tale of Two Cities* takes place in the years _____ the French Revolution.
   - ❏ a. before and after
   - ❏ b. during and after
   - ❏ c. before and during

2. In reading *A Tale of Two Cities,* one notices that Dickens
   - ❏ a. includes only accurate details of the Revolution.
   - ❏ b. at times distorts some details of the French Revolution.
   - ❏ c. wrote a completely fictional book that includes no facts about the French Revolution.

3. Dickens's description of the storming of the Bastille omits mentioning that the mob was looking for
   - ❏ a. the king's troops.
   - ❏ b. ammunition to defend themselves with.
   - ❏ c. nobles who disagreed with their position.

4. Dickens's character the Marquis represents the
   - ❏ a. king's brother.
   - ❏ b. kindhearted nobles.
   - ❏ c. nobles who mistreated the lower classes.

5. Dickens's brief mention of France's spending
   - ❏ a. states the theme of *A Tale of Two Cities.*
   - ❏ b. is unimportant to an understanding of what caused the revolution.
   - ❏ c. reflects what is perhaps the major cause of the French Revolution.

Understanding Ideas

6. One can infer that, in order to pay its debts, the French government
   - ❏ a. abolished taxes.
   - ❏ b. frequently raised taxes.
   - ❏ c. lowered taxes on a regular basis.

7. It is likely that one cause of the revolution was
   - ❏ a. a lack of food.
   - ❏ b. the use of the guillotine.
   - ❏ c. a lack of ammunition.

8. One can conclude that most of the people executed during the French Revolution were members of the
   - ❏ a. nobility.
   - ❏ b. clergy.
   - ❏ c. middle and lower classes.

9. One can conclude that, if one wants to learn about the French Revolution, *A Tale of Two Cities*
   - ❏ a. is not a reliable source of information.
   - ❏ b. provides an accurate account of the entire French Revolution.
   - ❏ c. is a historic account of a few years during the French Revolution.

10. The author of this passage seems _____ Dickens's historical inaccuracies in *A Tale of Two Cities.*
    - ❏ a. approving of
    - ❏ b. critical of
    - ❏ c. indifferent to

When Marie Antoinette married the crown prince of France, she was 14 years old, and he was 15. Four years later, in 1774, her husband became king of France, and she became queen. Born in Vienna, Marie Antoinette was the daughter of Empress Maria Theresa and Emperor Francis I, rulers of the Holy Roman Empire, which included the present-day countries of Austria and Germany.

When Marie Antoinette arrived in France, many French referred to her derisively as "the Austrian." She was an outsider, and therefore they disliked her. Nor did her frivolous ways endear her to the population. As queen, she entertained lavishly, ignoring France's financial crisis and dismissing those who tried to curb her spending. People called her Madame Deficit. They told untrue stories about her, including one in which, after learning that the people of Paris had no bread and were starving, she reputedly answered, "Then let them eat cake." The poor believed this tale, and their dislike grew.

After the revolution began, a crowd stormed the palace and captured the royal family. The queen tried to obtain aid from other European rulers and later attempted to flee from France with her family. Revolutionaries recaptured them. Shortly thereafter, the revolutionaries abolished the monarchy, imprisoned the royal family, and beheaded the king, the queen, and their son.

1. **Recognizing Words in Context**

   Find the word *derisively* in the passage. One definition below is closest to the meaning of that word. One definition has the opposite or nearly the opposite meaning. The remaining definition has a completely different meaning. Label the definitions C for *closest*, O for *opposite or nearly opposite*, and D for *different*.

   _____ a. rarely

   _____ b. scornfully

   _____ c. respectfully

2. **Distinguishing Fact from Opinion**

   Two of the statements below present *facts*, which can be proved. The other statement is an *opinion*, which expresses someone's thoughts or beliefs. Label the statements F for *fact* and O for *opinion*.

   _____ a. Marie Antoinette was a cruel person.

   _____ b. Marie Antoinette became queen in 1774.

   _____ c. Marie Antoinette entertained.

3. Keeping Events in Order

Number the statements below 1, 2, and 3 to show the order in which the events took place.

_____ a. Revolutionaries beheaded the queen.

_____ b. The queen and her family attempted to flee from France.

_____ c. A crowd stormed the palace and captured the royal family.

4. Making Correct Inferences

Two of the statements below are correct *inferences*, or reasonable guesses. They are based on information in the passage. The other statement is an incorrect, or faulty, inference. Label the statements C for *correct* inference and F for *faulty* inference.

_____ a. Marie Antoinette was an unpopular queen.

_____ b. Marie Antoinette caused France's financial crisis.

_____ c. Marie Antoinette was blamed for France's financial problems.

5. Understanding Main Ideas

One of the statements below expresses the main idea of the passage. One statement is too general, or too broad. The other explains only part of the passage; it is too narrow. Label the statements M for *main idea*, B for *too broad*, and N for *too narrow*.

_____ a. Many French referred to Marie Antoinette as "the Austrian."

_____ b. Blamed for France's financial woes, Marie Antoinette was an unpopular queen who was beheaded during the revolution.

_____ c. Marie Antoinette was an eighteenth-century European monarch.

Correct Answers, Part A _____

Correct Answers, Part B _____

Total Correct Answers _____

On October 8, 1871, much of Chicago became an inferno. The fire began in or near the O'Leary family's barn. No one knows for certain how it started, but it developed into a conflagration that consumed miles of the city, killed about three hundred people, and left about one hundred thousand homeless. Many conditions may have contributed to the Great Chicago Fire.

Dry weather was one possible factor. The summer and autumn had been unusually dry, and 20 fires occurred the week before the Great Fire. Just the night before, the city's firefighters battled a severe blaze, and many were exhausted. Besides firefighters' being fatigued, the Chicago Fire Department was understaffed and inadequately equipped.

Also, most buildings were wooden, and many were crowded together. Even sidewalks were wooden, and rooftops were of shingles or tar—both flammable materials. Interspersed between residences were warehouses and businesses, some containing paint and other flammable merchandise.

Although a citizen had allegedly sounded an alarm, the central alarm office had no record of it. Possibly the alarm malfunctioned. To make things worse, a watchman scanning the skies for fires misjudged the location and sent an alarm that caused firefighters to rush to an incorrect site. Realizing his error, the watchman tried to send a second alarm, but the telegraph dispatcher refused to allow it, fearing that it would confuse the firefighters. These errors caused the fire to grow quickly out of control before firefighters reached the scene.

Lacking telephones, radio, and television in 1871, few people in Chicago realized the severity of the fire until they had to scramble to escape it. Some people rushed into Lake Michigan to escape the flames, while others fled to the prairie or elsewhere. Meanwhile, troops and civilians blew up buildings to create a firebreak, hoping that it would contain the fire or, at least, slow its progress.

Strong winds blew burning embers onto buildings and across the Chicago River, causing the fire to spread still farther. The fire ignited oil and boats floating on the water and caused the gasworks to explode. It burned the wooden roof of the waterworks, which collapsed and destroyed the city's water pumps. Unless firefighters could pump water from the river or lake, they were helpless to stop the blaze. Just when it appeared that nothing would stop the inferno that roared through the city, rain fell on October 10 and contained the fire.

Reading Time _____

Recalling Facts

1. At the time of the Great Chicago Fire, the Chicago Fire Department
   - ❏ a. had more equipment than staff.
   - ❏ b. had too many unskilled fire-fighters.
   - ❏ c. was understaffed and inadequately equipped.

2. The Great Chicago Fire began
   - ❏ a. at the city gasworks.
   - ❏ b. in or near the O'Leary family's barn.
   - ❏ c. in a warehouse several miles from Lake Michigan.

3. Few people realized the severity of the fire until
   - ❏ a. after it ended.
   - ❏ b. they had to escape it.
   - ❏ c. they reached the water.

4. Strong winds caused the fire to
   - ❏ a. go out.
   - ❏ b. cool down.
   - ❏ c. spread.

5. Troops and civilians blew up buildings
   - ❏ a. by mistake.
   - ❏ b. to create a firebreak.
   - ❏ c. to signal the location of the fire.

Understanding Ideas

6. One can conclude that the fire spread rapidly as a result of
   - ❏ a. natural factors and human error.
   - ❏ b. laziness on the part of the firefighters.
   - ❏ c. skillful planning by experienced arsonists.

7. It is likely that the fire would not have spread so quickly if
   - ❏ a. the sun had been shining.
   - ❏ b. high winds had been blowing.
   - ❏ c. the summer and autumn had been wet.

8. The fire department resources proved to be _____ for fighting the fire.
   - ❏ a. adequate
   - ❏ b. deficient
   - ❏ c. exceptional

9. One can conclude that less damage might have occurred if
   - ❏ a. the dry weather had continued.
   - ❏ b. people had left the city immediately.
   - ❏ c. there had been more effective communication systems.

10. One way to prevent a similar disaster from occurring would be to
    - ❏ a. decrease the size of the fire department.
    - ❏ b. rebuild the city just as it was before the fire.
    - ❏ c. use fire-resistant materials to construct buildings.

18   B   Rebuilding Chicago

In the aftermath of the Great Chicago Fire of 1871, much of the city lay smoldering. Buildings that had survived the flames stood unscathed, but the fire had destroyed about eighteen thousand structures.

Almost at once, the residents of Chicago began rebuilding their ruined city. They cleared away rubble, and a relief committee distributed donated lumber and other supplies so that people could build temporary shelters. Some people even set up stands and started businesses.

Within six weeks, workers began erecting more than 200 new stone and brick buildings. By the end of 1871, people had built thousands of wooden structures and nearly 500 brick or stone buildings. Ultimately planners would increase the size of the shopping area and separate business and residential areas.

In 1873 a bank failure caused an economic depression, and most building was halted. Then, in 1874, a fire destroyed more than 800 buildings. As a result, the city improved its fire department and adopted stricter building codes, such as limiting the use of flammable materials.

The slowdown in building gave architects time to plan a style of buildings that people called the "Chicago school." These newer, safer buildings featured steel girders and brick or granite facing and included the first metal-frame skyscrapers, a design that soon would appear around the world.

1. **Recognizing Words in Context**

   Find the word *unscathed* in the passage. One definition below is closest to the meaning of that word. One definition has the opposite or nearly the opposite meaning. The remaining definition has a completely different meaning. Label the definitions C for *closest*, O for *opposite or nearly opposite*, and D for *different*.

   _____ a. ruined

   _____ b. burning

   _____ c. intact

2. **Distinguishing Fact from Opinion**

   Two of the statements below present *facts*, which can be proved. The other statement is an *opinion*, which expresses someone's thoughts or beliefs. Label the statements F for *fact* and O for *opinion*.

   _____ a. The relief committee distributed supplies to build temporary shelters.

   _____ b. The "Chicago school" was a new style of building.

   _____ c. The new skyscrapers were more beautiful than the buildings destroyed in the Great Chicago Fire.

3. **Keeping Events in Order**

   Number the statements below 1, 2, and 3 to show the order in which the events took place.

   _____ a. By the end of 1871, people had built thousands of wooden structures.

   _____ b. A bank failure caused a depression.

   _____ c. Architects planned a new style of building.

4. **Making Correct Inferences**

   Two of the statements below are correct *inferences,* or reasonable guesses. They are based on information in the passage. The other statement is an incorrect, or faulty, inference. Label the statements C for *correct* inference and F for *faulty* inference.

   _____ a. Before the economic depression of 1873, people were making a serious effort to build less flammable structures.

   _____ b. The fire of 1874 destroyed many buildings because they were made of wood.

   _____ c. The buildings of the Chicago school were safer because they were made of materials that were more fire resistant.

5. **Understanding Main Ideas**

   One of the statements below expresses the main idea of the passage. One statement is too general, or too broad. The other explains only part of the passage; it is too narrow. Label the statements M for *main idea*, B for *too broad*, and N for *too narrow.*

   _____ a. Firefighters in large cities learned important information from fire-related experiences and adjusted fire codes accordingly.

   _____ b. Skyscrapers were a new feature in the rebuilt Chicago.

   _____ c. After the Great Chicago Fire, the city eventually was rebuilt with fire safety in mind, and a new architectural style developed.

Correct Answers, Part A _____

Correct Answers, Part B _____

Total Correct Answers _____

Some 25 centuries before Columbus set sail across the Atlantic Ocean, people on the other side of the world navigated across the vast Pacific Ocean to settle on far-flung islands. European explorers first ventured into the South Pacific in 1595. As they explored, they found islands inhabited by people who used simple Stone Age tools. They could not believe such people had managed to sail such great distances, so the Europeans devised fanciful theories about how the islands were settled.

Fancy gave way to scientific thought with the expeditions of Captain James Cook in the late eighteenth century. Cook and his team of scientists, including a botanist named Joseph Banks, immersed themselves in several of the cultures in what is now called Polynesia (from the Greek for "many islands"). Cook and Banks discovered that the languages on these islands were remarkably similar. They also found strong similarities between these Polynesian languages and the languages in Southeast Asia. Their findings have since been confirmed, and the name Austronesian has been given to this group of related languages.

In the period between World Wars I and II, scientists flocked to the South Pacific. They were looking for archaeological evidence to support the Southeast Asia theory and to establish migration routes. Findings were debated, and challenges to the theory arose. The best known came from Norwegian explorer Thor Heyerdahl. In the mid-1940s, he proposed that South America was the point of origin and that the major migration route moved westward with ocean currents. Further evidence came in the form of Lapita ware, pottery that had been discovered on several islands. It could be dated and compared across sites. In addition, as more and more islands were studied, domesticated animals and crops found there were linked to Southeast Asia—all but the sweet potato. This Polynesian staple, native to South America, was the only real support for Heyerdahl's theory.

Most scientists agree that the evidence overwhelmingly supports a major eastward migration from Southeast Asia to New Guinea. From there the route led southeast through the islands known as Micronesia and Melanesia. From these islands, the route extended farther east to the Polynesian islands of Fiji, Tonga, and Samoa. These islands, in turn, launched voyages farther south, north, and east—possibly as far east as South America (which would account for the sweet potatoes). More studies are needed to trace fully the routes of these early masters of the sea.

Reading Time _____

Recalling Facts

1. People first began navigating the Pacific Ocean
   - ❏ a. in 1595.
   - ❏ b. about ten thousand years ago.
   - ❏ c. more than twenty-five hundred years ago.

2. Most scientists believe that the early Polynesians came from
   - ❏ a. South America.
   - ❏ b. Southeast Asia.
   - ❏ c. the South Pacific.

3. Most of the evidence that supports an eastward migration route was found
   - ❏ a. after World War I.
   - ❏ b. in the mid-1940s.
   - ❏ c. in the eighteenth century.

4. The only piece of evidence found in Polynesia that supports a westward migration route is
   - ❏ a. Lapita ware.
   - ❏ b. the sweet potato.
   - ❏ c. the type of boat used.

5. Cook's team concluded that the Polynesians were linked to a particular point of origin because of similarities in
   - ❏ a. crops.
   - ❏ b. language.
   - ❏ c. domesticated animals.

Understanding Ideas

6. It is likely that early European explorers believed the Polynesians to be
   - ❏ a. master sailors.
   - ❏ b. easygoing and friendly.
   - ❏ c. simple and not very bright.

7. Early Europeans' misconceptions about Polynesians were based on
   - ❏ a. their language.
   - ❏ b. the tools they used.
   - ❏ c. the boats they made.

8. One can infer that the reaction of the scientific community to Thor Heyerdahl's theory was
   - ❏ a. little or no support.
   - ❏ b. overwhelming support.
   - ❏ c. anger that their theory was challenged.

9. It is reasonable to conclude that the ancient Polynesians
   - ❏ a. were especially skilled at farming.
   - ❏ b. were the first to domesticate the sweet potato.
   - ❏ c. had great skill in shipbuilding and navigating.

10. One can infer that scientists
    - ❏ a. are considering the theory that the sweet potato may have originated in Asia.
    - ❏ b. continue to explore islands for evidence related to migration patterns.
    - ❏ c. have concluded that they know all they need to know about settlement of the South Pacific.

Kon-Tiki: Following in the Wake of Ancient Navigators

On April 28, 1947, six men set out to cover thousands of miles of open ocean in a large raft made of nine balsa logs. This expedition was intended to prove a theory of its leader, Thor Heyerdahl (1914–2002). While studying wildlife on a Polynesian island, Heyerdahl became convinced that its original settlers had embarked from South America. The scientific community disagreed, claiming that ancient sailors could not have navigated huge stretches of ocean on their simple rafts.

Heyerdahl set out to prove that such a feat was possible. He chose five companions on the basis of skills and temperament. He wanted calm sailors whose sanguine natures could withstand the challenges of three or four months at sea. He and his crew carefully built their craft along the lines of a prehistoric South American raft. Unlike on the ancients' craft, a radio was onboard in case of emergencies.

The *Kon-Tiki* raft, named for the Polynesian hero-god Tiki, sailed more than 4,000 miles, from Callao, Peru, to the island Angatau in the South Pacific. Landing proved to be difficult, however. The *Kon-Tiki* drifted for a few days before crashing on a coral reef, with crew uninjured.

Heyerdahl's intriguing theories never were accepted, but the best-selling book he wrote about the expedition, *Kon-Tiki,* made him a beloved and celebrated world figure.

1. **Recognizing Words in Context**

   Find the word *sanguine* in the passage. One definition below is closest to the meaning of that word. One definition has the opposite or nearly the opposite meaning. The remaining definition has a completely different meaning. Label the definitions C for *closest,* O for *opposite or nearly opposite,* and D for *different.*

   _____ a. cheerful

   _____ b. gloomy

   _____ c. combative

2. **Distinguishing Fact from Opinion**

   Two of the statements below present *facts,* which can be proved. The other statement is an *opinion,* which expresses someone's thoughts or beliefs. Label the statements F for *fact* and O for *opinion.*

   _____ a. Thor Heyerdahl's book about his expedition was a best-seller.

   _____ b. Heyerdahl's theories about Polynesian settlers were intriguing.

   _____ c. Unlike ancient rafts, the *Kon-Tiki* had a radio onboard.

3. Keeping Events in Order

Number the statements below 1, 2, and 3 to show the order in which the events took place.

_____ a. Heyerdahl formulated a theory about the original Polynesian settlers.

_____ b. Heyerdahl arrived on a Polynesian island to study its wildlife.

_____ c. Six men embarked on the *Kon-Tiki* expedition from Peru to the South Pacific.

4. Making Correct Inferences

Two of the statements below are correct *inferences,* or reasonable guesses. They are based on information in the passage. The other statement is an incorrect, or faulty, inference. Label the statements C for *correct* inference and F for *faulty* inference.

_____ a. Early South American seagoing rafts were made from balsa wood.

_____ b. The *Kon-Tiki* expedition is celebrated for its adventurousness, not for its scientific breakthroughs.

_____ c. Heyerdahl based his theory on rigorous scientific investigation.

5. Understanding Main Ideas

One of the statements below expresses the main idea of the passage. One statement is too general, or too broad. The other explains only part of the passage; it is too narrow. Label the statements M for *main idea,* B for *too broad,* and N for *too narrow.*

_____ a. Thor Heyerdahl's *Kon-Tiki* navigated more than 4,000 miles of open ocean.

_____ b. Thor Heyerdahl is a beloved, celebrated world figure.

_____ c. Thor Heyerdahl's *Kon-Tiki* expedition, although successful, did not accomplish what its leader had intended.

Correct Answers, Part A _____

Correct Answers, Part B _____

Total Correct Answers _____

Alexis de Tocqueville's View of Democracy in America

Alexis de Tocqueville was a prominent nineteenth-century French politician and writer. A liberal who believed in personal freedom, he also was an early activist for democracy. In 1831 he visited the United States to study its politics and its social life. At that time, most countries in Europe were ruled by monarchs, but this was changing as people called for more rights and representation. Democracy was stirring in Europe, and many eyes were watching the progress of the United States, the young nation forging its own future.

Tocqueville's acclaimed book *Democracy in America* captured his observations about the growth of democracy in the United States, just 50 years after its independence. He was impressed by what he found. He hoped to transfer some of its concepts to France and other countries. He was most impressed by the equality and self-rule Americans enjoyed.

Tocqueville wrote, "Nothing struck me more forcibly than the general equality of condition among the people." He found many signs of equality: people's style of clothing, their politeness to each other, their average income and level of education, and other social and economic factors. In Europe laws and social customs made it difficult for a person to rise socially or economically. In the United States, people had better access to education, greater choices of trade or profession, and more opportunities to succeed.

Equality and education are vital to the success of government by the people, for the people. Tocqueville was thrilled by the involvement of the American people in their governing and lawmaking. He called it "the sovereignty of the people," or people's ability to govern themselves. At that time, the United States was the only country in which a citizen could have a voice in making the laws. The people also elected their town, county, and state officials and national representatives and leaders. No citizens had ever had such power and freedom.

However, Tocqueville realized that the country's equality and opportunity were limited to men of European descent. Women did not have the rights of men, and Native Americans were not allowed to participate in the democracy. At that time, slavery was still practiced in the South, excluding most African Americans from the rights of citizenship. He clearly believed in the power of democracy to achieve new equalities: "It creates opinions, gives birth to new sentiments, founds novel customs, and modifies whatever it does not produce."

Reading Time _____

Recalling Facts

1. Alexis de Tocqueville was a
   - ❏ a. liberal English visitor.
   - ❏ b. liberal French politician.
   - ❏ c. conservative French author.

2. When Tocqueville wrote his book,
   - ❏ a. Europeans took little interest in the United States.
   - ❏ b. most Europeans supported the absolute power of monarchs.
   - ❏ c. the idea of democracy was gaining popular support in Europe.

3. At the time Tocqueville wrote his book, most European countries were
   - ❏ a. monarchies.
   - ❏ b. monopolies.
   - ❏ c. democracies.

4. Tocqueville was favorably impressed by the
   - ❏ a. degree of equality among Americans.
   - ❏ b. discrepancy between rich and poor in America.
   - ❏ c. similarities between European and American social structures.

5. When Tocqueville wrote *Democracy in America,*
   - ❏ a. all Americans enjoyed the same rights of citizenship.
   - ❏ b. the full rights of citizenship were not extended to every American.
   - ❏ c. all Americans except Native Americans and enslaved persons enjoyed the same rights of citizenship.

Understanding Ideas

6. Compared with Europeans of Tocqueville's day, Americans were
   - ❏ a. more stylishly dressed.
   - ❏ b. less concerned with class distinctions.
   - ❏ c. less involved with political decision making.

7. Tocqueville was thrilled with what he called "the sovereignty of the people" in contrast to the sovereignty of
   - ❏ a. the nobility.
   - ❏ b. the middle class.
   - ❏ c. a single head of state.

8. Democracy was considered revolutionary because it
   - ❏ a. was a change of government.
   - ❏ b. distributed power among the citizens.
   - ❏ c. could only be achieved through violent acts and war.

9. Tocqueville saw democracy as realized in America
   - ❏ a. to be fundamentally flawed.
   - ❏ b. as a perfect form of government.
   - ❏ c. as a model that he hoped would inspire changes in his own and other countries.

10. According to Tocqueville, democracy is not only a type of government but also
   - ❏ a. a creative force.
   - ❏ a. the key to happiness.
   - ❏ a. an ideal that will never be fully realized.

Tocqueville's View of Prisons

When French writer Alexis de Tocqueville set out for the United States in 1831, he was not examining just the development of democracy. The French government had asked him to review the prison system in America and to recommend reforms for prisons in France.

According to Tocqueville, the goals of imprisonment are to reform and to instill productive habits. Three aspects of U.S. prisons were conducive to these goals: labor, silence, and solitude.

In most prisons, inmates performed manual labor and maintained strict silence throughout the day. It was thought that solitude of the mind, enforced by the rule of silence, let prisoners reflect and achieve moral reformation. Also, silence helped maintain order and obedience, two important habits for productive members of society.

There were two schools of thought on prisons' use of solitude. In Pennsylvania one prison kept inmates separated at all times. They ate, slept, and worked alone, never mingling with other prisoners. In other facilities, prisoners would eat and sleep in individual cells but would work in groups. Solitary confinement was sometimes used as a punishment, but Tocqueville disagreed with this method, saying that it endangered the health of the inmate. He agreed, however, with the use of the whip and other forms of corporal punishment to maintain discipline.

1. **Recognizing Words in Context**

Find the word *conducive* in the passage. One definition below is closest to the meaning of that word. One definition has the opposite or nearly the opposite meaning. The remaining definition has a completely different meaning. Label the definitions C for *closest*, O for *opposite or nearly opposite*, and D for *different*.

_____ a. preventive

_____ b. helpful

_____ c. unpleasant

2. **Distinguishing Fact from Opinion**

Two of the statements below present *facts*, which can be proved. The other statement is an *opinion*, which expresses someone's thoughts or beliefs. Label the statements F for *fact* and O for *opinion*.

_____ a. Tocqueville was asked to examine prisons in America.

_____ b. Tocqueville found two theories of prisons' use of solitude.

_____ c. Solitary confinement endangers the health of prisoners.

3. Keeping Events in Order

Number the statements below 1, 2, and 3 to show the order in which the events took place.

_____ a. Tocqueville made recommendations to the French government on prison reform.

_____ b. Tocqueville refined his opinions on the value of different aspects of prison life.

_____ c. Tocqueville toured prisons throughout the United States.

4. Making Correct Inferences

Two of the statements below are correct *inferences,* or reasonable guesses. They are based on information in the passage. The other statement is an incorrect, or faulty, inference. Label the statements C for *correct* inference and F for *faulty* inference.

_____ a. Tocqueville believed that imprisonment needed only to instill labor, silence, and solitude in order to succeed in reforming all prisoners.

_____ b. Tocqueville wanted prisoners to become useful members of society.

_____ c. Tocqueville was concerned about criminals' moral well-being.

5. Understanding Main Ideas

One of the statements below expresses the main idea of the passage. One statement is too general, or too broad. The other explains only part of the passage; it is too narrow. Label the statements M for *main idea*, B for *too broad*, and N for *too narrow.*

_____ a. Alexis de Tocqueville thought that prisoners should be required to perform manual labor.

_____ b. In his study of prisons in the United States for the French government, Alexis de Tocqueville found three noteworthy ideas—labor, silence, and solitude—that contributed to prisoner reform.

_____ c. Prison reform was a goal of the French government in the first half of the nineteenth century.

Correct Answers, Part A _____

Correct Answers, Part B _____

Total Correct Answers _____

Great Britain's Empire

Imperialism is the process of building an empire, with weaker groups being taken over by stronger ones. Sometimes this is done through military means and sometimes through economic pressure. Most often empires impose their own culture and traditions on the societies they take over. Being part of an empire may include benefits, but it can also cause problems. Great Britain once built an empire, over the course of hundreds of years, that circled the globe.

During the 1500s, English merchants founded trading posts in the lands across the Atlantic Ocean. As the European demand for products such as sugar, tobacco, and timber grew, England claimed these regions to protect its financial interests. Although it lost its colonies in North America in the late 1700s, the British Empire continued to grow.

Australia, New Zealand, and India were the next lands to be annexed. They provided products for the marketplace and safe harbors where ships might anchor for rest, repairs, and replenishment. Great Britain also colonized Africa and Asia. In the early 1900s, British possessions were so vast that it could be said that "the sun never set on" the empire. It occupied four million square miles on six continents, or about one quarter of the world's area. About a quarter of the world's population was considered British.

Empire building almost always brings with it social and political unrest. So it was for Great Britain. Conquered peoples resented their overlords. The descendents of settlers also grew unhappy with British rule. The British government's response to these problems took two main forms: Where there were large numbers of emigrants from Great Britain, it often turned over the reins of government to the people. Countries such as Australia and Canada were allowed to rule themselves as dominions of the empire. In places where native peoples outnumbered British immigrants, on the other hand, Great Britain took tighter control. Countries such as India and China, and those in Africa, were ruled by governors sent from Great Britain.

Revolt and even war were common in the empire, even in countries as different as Ireland and China. In 1931 Great Britain put an end to the empire when it declared itself a commonwealth of nations. Now many former dominions are independent countries. India and Pakistan gained independence in 1947. The Republic of Ireland was declared in 1949. Hong Kong, a British possession since 1840, was returned to China in 1997.

Reading Time _____

Recalling Facts

1. Imperialism is
   - ❏ a. the process of building an empire.
   - ❏ b. a good approach to helping weaker nations.
   - ❏ c. a description of a commonwealth of nations.

2. The British empire began in the 1500s, when
   - ❏ a. Great Britain lost its colonies in North America.
   - ❏ b. Great Britain found safe harbors in Australia where ships could anchor.
   - ❏ c. merchants founded trading posts in the lands across the Atlantic Ocean.

3. Empire building almost always brings with it
   - ❏ a. social and political unrest.
   - ❏ b. a better form of government.
   - ❏ c. an improved economy for the conquered peoples.

4. Countries such as Canada, which had large numbers of British immigrants,
   - ❏ a. resented their overlords.
   - ❏ b. stayed under the rule of governors sent out from Great Britain.
   - ❏ c. were allowed to rule themselves as dominions of the empire.

5. Great Britain put an end to the empire in 1931, when it
   - ❏ a. returned Hong Kong to China.
   - ❏ b. declared itself a commonwealth of nations.
   - ❏ c. granted independence to India and Pakistan.

Understanding Ideas

6. It was said that the sun never set on the British Empire because
   - ❏ a. the British were loved and admired wherever they went.
   - ❏ b. it was thought that the empire would endure forever.
   - ❏ c. it spanned the globe, so it was always daytime in some part of it.

7. When a country is annexed by an empire, it is
   - ❏ a. taken over completely.
   - ❏ b. regarded as an equal partner.
   - ❏ c. allowed to make independent decisions about the economy.

8. One could infer that, during the time of its empire, the British government
   - ❏ a. cared little about trade matters.
   - ❏ b. encouraged the dominions to work toward independence.
   - ❏ c. believed that the native peoples were not able to govern themselves.

9. Imperialism is likely to be motivated by a desire to
   - ❏ a. gain and protect economic advantage.
   - ❏ b. bring democratic government to people worldwide.
   - ❏ c. improve health and education in poor countries.

10. Which of the following sentences best expresses the main idea?
   - ❏ a. Stronger nations have always tried to take over weaker ones.
   - ❏ b. Hong Kong, a British possession, was returned to China in 1997.
   - ❏ c. The British built an empire that grew to include a quarter of the world's area and people.

The Boxer Rebellion was an attempt to purge China of foreigners and their culture. Since the early 1800s, the country had been the target of foreign imperialism and greed, a policy known as "carving up the Chinese melon." By the 1890s, the country was poor and in turmoil. Power and wealth were concentrated in very few hands. Most people lived in poverty.

The Boxers emerged in the late 1890s as champions of Chinese tradition, calling themselves the Fists of Righteousness and Harmony. This secret group performed ritual magic intended to make them unassailable— safe from bullets and untouched by pain. They also practiced the martial arts, hence the Western name Boxers. The Boxers roamed the countryside, killing foreigners, missionaries, and Chinese converts to Christianity.

In 1900, at the urging of the empress, the Boxers attacked the northern cities of Beijing and Tientsin. Almost two months later, the rampage was quelled by a relief force of European, Japanese, and American troops. The final death toll included tens of thousands of Chinese and perhaps a thousand foreigners.

The peace treaty of 1901 further weakened China. It was forced to pay huge sums in penalties and to allow foreign troops to be stationed there. Access to China's natural resources and control over many of its industries were given to foreign interests.

1. **Recognizing Words in Context**

Find the word *unassailable* in the passage. One definition below is closest to the meaning of that word. One definition has the opposite or nearly the opposite meaning. The remaining definition has a completely different meaning. Label the definitions C for *closest*, O for *opposite or nearly opposite*, and D for *different*.

_____ a. vulnerable

_____ b. refined

_____ c. indestructible

2. **Distinguishing Fact from Opinion**

Two of the statements below present *facts*, which can be proved. The other statement is an *opinion*, which expresses someone's thoughts or beliefs. Label the statements F for *fact* and O for *opinion*.

_____ a. The Boxers were justified in their attacks on foreigners.

_____ b. The name Boxers relates to the group's practice of the martial arts.

_____ c. The Boxer Rebellion was an attempt to make all foreigners leave China.

3. **Keeping Events in Order**

Number the statements below 1, 2, and 3 to show the order in which the events took place.

_____ a. China was forced to pay a heavy penalty for the Boxer Rebellion.

_____ b. European nations practiced a policy known as "carving up the Chinese melon."

_____ c. A group formed in China called the Fists of Righteousness and Harmony.

4. **Making Correct Inferences**

Two of the statements below are correct *inferences,* or reasonable guesses. They are based on information in the passage. The other statement is an incorrect, or faulty, inference. Label the statements C for *correct* inference and F for *faulty* inference.

_____ a. Great wealth was to be made from China's natural resources and industrial development in the nineteenth century.

_____ b. China had welcomed the interest of Western nations at first.

_____ c. The Boxers believed that the presence of foreigners in China was bringing about the destruction of their culture.

5. **Understanding Main Ideas**

One of the statements below expresses the main idea of the passage. One statement is too general, or too broad. The other explains only part of the passage; it is too narrow. Label the statements M for *main idea,* B for *too broad,* and N for *too narrow.*

_____ a. The Boxer Rebellion attempted but failed to dislodge the presence of foreign interests in China.

_____ b. The Boxers called themselves the Fists of Righteousness and Harmony.

_____ c. China is a large country with many natural resources and a culture very different from that of Europe.

Correct Answers, Part A _____

Correct Answers, Part B _____

Total Correct Answers _____

The Right Attorney for the Right Job

An attorney is an agent authorized to act for a person or concern. An attorney at law, or lawyer, is an officer of a court of law who acts as an agent in legal proceedings. This means that lawyers must serve two masters. One master is the client. Lawyers use the law and the legal system to protect and serve the needs of clients. The other master is the law itself. Lawyers must uphold the law, which is based on the U.S. Constitution, written legislation, and past court decisions.

Almost all aspiring lawyers attend a law school approved by the bar association of the state in which they want to practice. A bar association is a professional group for lawyers. The term *bar* is taken from the historic structure of a courtroom. A lawyer who had "passed the bar" could step beyond the bar or railing that separated members of the public from those involved in proceedings. Each state offers its own bar examination. Some states recognize attorneys qualified elsewhere, but most states require attorneys to pass that state's bar exam before they can practice there.

The law is extremely complex and changes constantly as new legislation is enacted and new interpretations win favorable rulings in the courts. Every aspect of life, from artistic production and sports to taxes and the environment, is a specialty area in law. Two specialties are corporate law and criminal law.

A corporate attorney handles legal matters for businesses. Much of this work involves transactions such as employment contracts, arrangements for loans, rental agreements, and mergers with other companies. Sometimes businesses must appear in court, in which case they need a corporate attorney who is also a litigator. Litigation is a dispute that is taken to court. A litigator files the lawsuit and helps the client resolve the dispute, either by negotiating a settlement or by presenting arguments in court.

In criminal law, prosecutors who work for the government try the case against a defendant accused of some crime. Defense lawyers represent the defendant at every step: from the first appearance in court for arraignment on charges, through a variety of proceedings including the trial and sentencing if the defendant is convicted, to appeals intended to reverse or modify an unfavorable decision. If a defendant is unable or unwilling to hire a lawyer, the court appoints a public defender, at no cost, to take the case.

Reading Time _____

Recalling Facts

1. A synonym for *attorney at law* is
   - ❑ a. bar.
   - ❑ b. lawyer.
   - ❑ c. litigator.

2. A corporate attorney
   - ❑ a. manages legal matters for businesses.
   - ❑ b. rarely deals with transactions such as contracts.
   - ❑ c. tries cases against defendants accused of crimes.

3. A public defender
   - ❑ a. is also known as a litigator.
   - ❑ b. tries the case against a defendant accused of some crime.
   - ❑ c. is appointed by the court when a person is unable to hire a private lawyer.

4. The bar is
   - ❑ a. an association of law schools.
   - ❑ b. a private social organization for lawyers.
   - ❑ c. named for the historic structure of a courtroom.

5. In the United States, the law is
   - ❑ a. written to protect clients and serve their needs.
   - ❑ b. based on the Constitution, written legislation, and past court decisions.
   - ❑ c. unlikely to change and is rarely open to different interpretations.

Understanding Ideas

6. It is likely that most states require lawyers to pass their own bar examinations because
   - ❑ a. areas of the law vary from state to state.
   - ❑ b. lawyers may not have studied hard in law school.
   - ❑ c. federal law does not always apply at the state level.

7. One could infer that a lawyer who has been disbarred
   - ❑ a. has been elevated to the role of judge.
   - ❑ b. is no longer permitted to practice law.
   - ❑ c. may not enter any part of a courtroom.

8. In the process of serving a client's needs, a lawyer
   - ❑ a. need only focus on those needs.
   - ❑ b. must do nothing that breaks or misrepresents the law.
   - ❑ c. has to think about what is best for everyone involved in the case.

9. If one wanted to build a factory and needed to borrow money, one would probably hire a
   - ❑ a. tax lawyer.
   - ❑ b. criminal lawyer.
   - ❑ c. corporate lawyer.

10. A good litigator
    - ❑ a. knows how to defend a client against criminal charges.
    - ❑ b. probably likes to argue and knows how to be persuasive.
    - ❑ c. is likely to spend more time on transactions than in the courtroom.

Jumping the Bar: Arabella Mansfield

Upon her admission to the Iowa bar in 1869, Arabella Mansfield became the first woman given official sanction to practice law in the United States. In fact, she was the first in Europe or North America. In Canada a woman was first admitted to the bar in 1897. France did not accept women lawyers until 1900. England and Ireland qualified their first women lawyers in 1922. Although Mansfield never argued a case in court or took on clients, she opened the door to women who would follow.

Mansfield was born Belle Aurelia Babb in Iowa in 1846. She studied law on her own and then passed the Iowa bar examination, despite a statute that limited admission to "white male" residents of the state. The Iowa Supreme Court ruled that language that appears to stipulate men can be understood to include women. What looked like a legal restriction could not be used to deny women admittance to the bar and therefore to the practice of law. This decision was cited in later court cases filed on behalf of women attempting to join the bar in other states.

Mansfield went on to a distinguished career as a college professor. She was also a founding member of the Iowa Woman Suffrage Society. She died in 1911 at the age of 65.

1. **Recognizing Words in Context**

   Find the word *stipulate* in the passage. One definition below is closest to the meaning of that word. One definition has the opposite or nearly the opposite meaning. The remaining definition has a completely different meaning. Label the definitions C for *closest*, O for *opposite or nearly opposite*, and D for *different*.

   _____ a. specify

   _____ b. precipitate

   _____ c. deny

2. **Distinguishing Fact from Opinion**

   Two of the statements below present *facts*, which can be proved. The other statement is an *opinion*, which expresses someone's thoughts or beliefs. Label the statements F for *fact* and O for *opinion*.

   _____ a. Arabella Mansfield was the first woman officially qualified to practice law in Europe or North America.

   _____ b. Mansfield was the most admired college professor.

   _____ c. Mansfield passed the Iowa bar examination after studying law on her own.

3. **Keeping Events in Order**

   Number the statements below 1, 2, and 3 to show the order in which the events took place.

   _____ a. Mansfield was admitted to the Iowa bar.

   _____ b. Mansfield helped found the Iowa Woman Suffrage Society.

   _____ c. The Iowa Supreme Court ruled that legal language that stipulates men can be understood to include women.

4. **Making Correct Inferences**

   Two of the statements below are correct *inferences*, or reasonable guesses. They are based on information in the passage. The other statement is an incorrect, or faulty, inference. Label the statements C for *correct* inference and F for *faulty* inference.

   _____ a. Various professions were not open to women in the nineteenth century.

   _____ b. Rules that govern the qualification of lawyers vary from state to state.

   _____ c. Mansfield was the first woman to practice law in the United States.

5. **Understanding Main Ideas**

   One of the statements below expresses the main idea of the passage. One statement is too general, or too broad. The other explains only part of the passage; it is too narrow. Label the statements M for *main idea*, B for *too broad*, and N for *too narrow*.

   _____ a. When Arabella Mansfield gained admission to the Iowa bar, she opened to other women the door to the legal profession.

   _____ b. Women in many countries were not admitted to the bar until the last half of the nineteenth and the early twentieth centuries.

   _____ c. Arabella Mansfield studied law on her own before she took and passed the Iowa bar exam.

Correct Answers, Part A _____

Correct Answers, Part B _____

Total Correct Answers _____

Roger Williams: A Man of Conscience

Roger Williams was a rare man of conscience—one who believed that all people should be free to practice the religion of their choice.

Williams, born in England, was ordained a minister in the Church of England, but he soon grew unhappy with the structure of the church. He believed that power over the church's members should not belong to a small group of bishops. Instead, he thought, each congregation should be allowed to manage its own affairs. Williams joined a group of like-minded people who called themselves Puritans, and in 1631 he and his family went to the American colonies.

Once there, he became a pastor and teacher. However, he soon discovered that the Puritan leadership of the Massachusetts Bay Colony had no intention of allowing the free practice of religion. Williams's ideas and outspoken ways got him into a great deal of trouble. In 1635 he was banished from the colony and almost forced to leave the colonies. He was able to elude the authorities, however, and traveled south into the territory of the Narragansett Nation.

Williams had challenged the leadership in Massachusetts on two key points. He claimed that the colonists had no right simply to take land. England, he said, could not claim territory as a colony without first buying it from the Native peoples who lived there. Williams then challenged the authority of the Puritans to control both religious and civil law, just as he had challenged the authority of the Church of England. He himself turned away from Puritanism and eventually became a "seeker," a person who embraced the beliefs of Christianity but did not follow a specific doctrine.

After Williams purchased land from the Narragansett, he received a charter from England that created the colony of Rhode Island. He set up a government based on tolerance and the complete separation of church and state. Among the early settlers who came there seeking religious freedom were the Quakers, or members of the Society of Friends. Williams disagreed with them on matters of faith, but he defended their right to practice Christianity according to their own set of beliefs. Williams extended freedom of religion to all, even to people who did not practice any form of Christianity. Although he continued throughout his life to preach the Word of God as he understood it, he gave up any attempt to convert the Native peoples to his own religion.

Reading Time _____

Recalling Facts

1. Roger Williams believed that
   - ❑ a. all people should be free to practice religion in their own way.
   - ❑ b. the church should be run by a small group of bishops.
   - ❑ c. freedom of religion should not extend to Native peoples.

2. Williams was ordained in the Church of England but
   - ❑ a. eventually lost his faith.
   - ❑ b. later became a member of the Society of Friends.
   - ❑ c. thought of himself as a Puritan for most of his life.

3. While living in the Massachusetts Bay Colony, Williams
   - ❑ a. was a successful Puritan pastor.
   - ❑ b. tried to take land from the Native peoples.
   - ❑ c. got into a great deal of trouble with the Puritan leadership.

4. When Williams was banished from the Massachusetts Bay Colony, he
   - ❑ a. was forced to leave America.
   - ❑ b. went west to convert Native peoples to his religion.
   - ❑ c. founded the colony of Rhode Island as a haven for those seeking religious freedom.

5. In Rhode Island, a key provision of Williams's government was
   - ❑ a. centralized authority.
   - ❑ b. complete separation of church and state.
   - ❑ c. the doctrine and beliefs of the Society of Friends.

Understanding Ideas

6. It seems likely that Roger Williams, when he immigrated to America,
   - ❑ a. expected to enjoy religious freedom.
   - ❑ b. hoped to support the ideas of the Church of England.
   - ❑ c. planned to dedicate his life to converting the Native peoples to Christianity.

7. The Puritan authorities wanted Williams to leave America because
   - ❑ a. he was encouraging the Native Americans to wage war.
   - ❑ b. he had threatened to take over the Massachusetts Bay Colony.
   - ❑ c. they were afraid that his ideas might influence Puritans to think independently.

8. Many of the early colonists
   - ❑ a. were not allowed to own land in America.
   - ❑ b. usually bought their land from the local Native Americans.
   - ❑ c. were granted ownership of the land from the English government.

9. Civil authorities
   - ❑ a. enforce laws made by the state.
   - ❑ b. focus on the rules of the church.
   - ❑ c. are members of a congregation.

10. Which of the following sentences best expresses the main idea?
    - ❑ a. Roger Williams and many early colonists sought religious freedom in America.
    - ❑ b. Roger Williams disagreed with the Quakers on matters of faith.
    - ❑ c. Roger Williams founded the colony of Rhode Island.

Puritanism was at first an effort to reform the Church of England. Some Puritans believed that this denomination simply needed to be "purified"; others wanted to separate from it completely. There was, however, widespread accord about the nature of good and evil. Puritans believed that human nature was sinful and that people needed the control of a strong authority. Self-discipline, hard work, and prayer were key virtues.

In the colonies, Puritanism was the center of the culture of the Massachusetts Bay Colony. The first Puritans arrived there in 1620. For more than 100 years, their religious outlook would shape civil law. The clergy could not hold public office, but members advised the people who did. Only members of the local Puritan church were allowed to vote.

Puritans left England in search of religious freedom. Uniformity in behavior and belief was their goal, and they considered the good of the community uppermost. The rigid enforcement of strict laws was thought to protect the community from both physical and moral danger, and penalties for transgressions were severe. Roger Williams, for instance, founded a colony in what is now the state of Rhode Island so as to escape Puritan persecution. The Quaker Mary Dyer was arrested three times for her beliefs, and after her fourth arrest in 1660, she was hanged.

1. **Recognizing Words in Context**

   Find the word *transgressions* in the passage. One definition below is closest to the meaning of that word. One definition has the opposite or nearly the opposite meaning. The remaining definition has a completely different meaning. Label the definitions C for *closest*, O for *opposite or nearly opposite*, and D for *different*.

   _____ a. message carriers

   _____ b. offenses

   _____ c. acts of obedience

2. **Distinguishing Fact from Opinion**

   Two of the statements below present *facts*, which can be proved. The other statement is an *opinion*, which expresses someone's thoughts or beliefs. Label the statements F for *fact* and O for *opinion*.

   _____ a. The Puritans' rigid enforcement of laws protected the community from physical and moral danger.

   _____ b. The Puritans believed that human nature was sinful.

   _____ c. In Puritan communities, only members of the church were allowed to vote.

3. Keeping Events in Order

Number the statements below 1, 2, and 3 to show the order in which the events took place.

_____ a. Mary Dyer was hanged for her Quaker beliefs.

_____ b. Puritans governed the Massachusetts Bay Colony.

_____ c. Puritans organized as a group in an effort to reform the Church of England.

4. Making Correct Inferences

Two of the statements below are correct *inferences,* or reasonable guesses. They are based on information in the passage. The other statement is an incorrect, or faulty, inference. Label the statements C for *correct* inference and F for *faulty* inference.

_____ a. Puritanism had less influence outside the Massachusetts Bay Colony than inside it.

_____ b. Puritans did not believe that people should be happy.

_____ c. Puritans were against the free exercise of religious beliefs.

5. Understanding Main Ideas

One of the statements below expresses the main idea of the passage. One statement is too general, or too broad. The other explains only part of the passage; it is too narrow. Label the statements M for *main idea*, B for *too broad*, and N for *too narrow.*

_____ a. Puritanism was a set of beliefs held by some Protestants.

_____ b. The strict enforcement of Puritan beliefs shaped the culture of colonial life in Massachusetts.

_____ c. Self-discipline and hard work were key Puritan virtues.

Correct Answers, Part A _____

Correct Answers, Part B _____

Total Correct Answers _____

Mongolia is a landlocked country located in northern Asia between two great world powers—Russia and China—each of which has exerted influence over it. Much of Mongolia consists of steppes, or dry, grass-covered plains. Although modern Mongolia has existed as a country only since the 1920s, people have inhabited Mongolia for thousands of years. These early Mongolians were nomadic hunters and herders, moving with their animals from place to place.

By the early 1200s, Genghis Khan, a Mongol chieftain, had united nomadic groups and trained them to become an efficient army. Genghis Khan and his troops conquered parts of China, central Asia, and parts of Europe to create a Mongol empire. Descendents of Genghis Khan continued to expand the empire, but in the late 1200s it began to disintegrate. About one hundred years later, it dissolved. By the late 1600s, China controlled Mongolia; in the early 1920s, Mongolia declared its independence. Thereafter, until 1990, Mongolia became dependent upon the Soviet Union for energy and economic aid.

Although increasing numbers of Mongolians work in industry, and nearly half the population lives in cities and towns, many Mongolians raise livestock, some of them living on livestock farms or ranches clustered around small towns. Today many Mongolians continue the nomadic herding tradition of their ancestors.

Herders tend goats, camels, yaks, sheep, cattle, and horses. They use the animals for food, clothing, and shelter. Herding families begin their chores early in the day. The women prepare the meals; milk any animals that require milking, such as camels, goats, and horses; make butter, cheese, and yogurt; sew clothes; and care for the household. The men herd the animals, driving them out to pasture in the morning and bringing them back at night, at which time the animals are again milked. Some Mongolians still herd their animals on horseback; others use motorcycles, jeeps, or other motorized vehicles.

Like their ancestors, many of today's nomads live in circular tents called *gers*. A tent suits the nomadic lifestyle because it is easy to erect, disassemble, and transport. A ger has a latticework frame and a wooden ceiling support covered with sturdy woolen felt, which the tent-owners fasten to the structure. Each tent has a brightly painted wooden door. Today iron stoves usually heat the tents, whereas in the past an open hearth warmed their interiors.

Reading Time _____

Recalling Facts

1. Modern Mongolia has existed as a country since the
   - ❏ a. 1200s.
   - ❏ b. 1920s.
   - ❏ c. 1990s.

2. The early Mongolians were
   - ❏ a. soldiers
   - ❏ b. industrialists.
   - ❏ c. nomadic hunters and herders.

3. Genghis Khan, a Mongol chieftain,
   - ❏ a. united the nomadic Mongol tribes.
   - ❏ b. controlled all of China and Europe.
   - ❏ c. began the industrialization of Mongolia.

4. Like their ancestors, many modern Mongolians
   - ❏ a. live in gers.
   - ❏ b. live in cities.
   - ❏ c. use iron stoves for heat.

5. One important tradition in today's Mongolia is
   - ❏ a. hunting.
   - ❏ b. nomadic herding.
   - ❏ c. building a strong army.

Understanding Ideas

6. Compared with the time of the Mongol empire, today's Mongolia is
   - ❏ a. larger.
   - ❏ b. about the same size.
   - ❏ c. considerably smaller.

7. One can infer that Mongolia
   - ❏ a. has easily defended borders.
   - ❏ b. is suitable mostly for agriculture.
   - ❏ c. is not surrounded by protective boundaries such as wide bodies of water or high mountains.

8. During most of the twentieth century, Mongolia was probably
   - ❏ a. self-sufficient.
   - ❏ b. a poor country.
   - ❏ c. a leader in specialized industries.

9. One can conclude that the lives of herding families have
   - ❏ a. remained unchanged.
   - ❏ b. changed somewhat over time.
   - ❏ c. changed substantially over time.

10. One can infer that the horse
   - ❏ a. originated in Mongolia.
   - ❏ b. continues to have an important place in Mongolian culture.
   - ❏ c. will soon disappear from Mongolia, replaced by motor vehicles.

Kublai Khan, Ruler of an Empire

Kublai Khan lived from 1215 to 1294. He was the grandson of Genghis Khan, who had established the Mongol empire. Like his grandfather, Kublai Khan was an emperor and a conqueror. He became ruler of the Mongol empire in 1260. During his reign, the Mongol empire reached its largest size, stretching from eastern Europe to eastern Asia. After conquering China, Kublai Khan established the Yuan dynasty, which lasted from 1279 to 1368. The Yuan dynasty marked the first time that foreigners ruled China.

Kublai Khan ruled his empire from China rather than Mongolia. Tolerant of most religious beliefs, he built schools, wrote new laws, reduced taxes, promoted trade, and used a pony-express-style message-relay system. He also ordered the construction of a new capital city, Daidu, which today is part of the Chinese capital of Beijing. Although he had Chinese advisors, the emperor distrusted the Chinese, perhaps because they had been enemies of the Mongols for many years. Therefore, he appointed Mongolians to top government positions and recruited foreigners to help govern his vast realm. He employed the Venetian merchant Marco Polo as a courier who relayed messages from the emperor to others.

Although Kublai Khan twice tried to invade Japan, his efforts to expand the Mongol empire farther eastward failed. Instead, he focused his attention on maintaining his empire.

1. Recognizing Words in Context

Find the word *recruited* in the passage. One definition below is closest to the meaning of that word. One definition has the opposite or nearly the opposite meaning. The remaining definition has a completely different meaning. Label the definitions C for *closest,* O for *opposite or nearly opposite,* and D for *different.*

_____ a. enlisted

_____ b. released

_____ c. attacked

2. Distinguishing Fact from Opinion

Two of the statements below present *facts,* which can be proved. The other statement is an *opinion,* which expresses someone's thoughts or beliefs. Label the statements F for *fact* and O for *opinion.*

_____ a. During Kublai Khan's reign, the Mongol empire reached its largest size.

_____ b. Kublai Khan employed Marco Polo as a courier.

_____ c. Kublai Khan was the greatest of the Mongol emperors.

3. **Keeping Events in Order**

Number the statements below 1, 2, and 3 to show the order in which the events took place.

_____ a. Kublai Khan established the Yuan dynasty.

_____ b. Kublai Khan became emperor of the Mongol empire.

_____ c. Kublai Khan conquered China.

4. **Making Correct Inferences**

Two of the statements below are correct *inferences*, or reasonable guesses. They are based on information in the passage. The other statement is an incorrect, or faulty, inference. Label the statements C for *correct* inference and F for *faulty* inference.

_____ a. Kublai Khan was a cautious man.

_____ b. Maintaining his empire was more important to Kublai Khan than expanding it.

_____ c. Throughout his reign, Kublai Khan was not interested in adding territory to his empire.

5. **Understanding Main Ideas**

One of the statements below expresses the main idea of the passage. One statement is too general, or too broad. The other explains only part of the passage; it is too narrow. Label the statements M for *main idea*, B for *too broad*, and N for *too narrow*.

_____ a. A good administrator and emperor, Kublai Khan expanded the Mongol empire and founded the Yuan dynasty.

_____ b. Kublai Khan was the first foreigner to rule China.

_____ c. Kublai Khan was one of China's great emperors.

Correct Answers, Part A _____

Correct Answers, Part B _____

Total Correct Answers _____

In 1787 the United States Constitution established the U.S. Supreme Court, the highest court in the nation. The Court's authority falls within two categories. In the first, it decides certain types of cases such as those involving U.S. officials or disputes between states. In its other capacity, it exercises appellate power and decides cases previously appealed in lower courts. Unlike those of the lower courts, rulings of the Supreme Court are final. Most Supreme Court cases fall within its appellate jurisdiction.

One of the main duties of this Court is to interpret the Constitution. In some cases, it has overruled state laws, thus asserting that the Constitution imparts greater authority to the Federal government than to the states. At other times, the Supreme Court has declared that states have the foremost power. Although rarely exercised, the Supreme Court has the power to determine whether an act of Congress is unconstitutional.

The Supreme Court has delivered many eminent rulings. One of the best known is *Brown v. Board of Education of Topeka* in 1954. In this famous case, the Court ruled that establishing separate schools according to race is contrary to the Constitution. Another renowned case is *Miranda* in which the Court ruled that officials making an arrest must advise that person of his or her rights.

The Supreme Court consists of a chief justice and eight associate justices. The president of the United States, with the approval of the Senate, appoints the justices, who serve until they retire or are impeached. Few justices have faced impeachment, and only one has been found guilty of wrongdoing. Because justices are not elected, they need not please voters. Usually they begin their careers as lawyers and later become judges in lower courts. In 1967 Thurgood Marshall became the first African American Supreme Court justice. Upon Marshall's retirement after more than 20 years of service, Clarence Thomas joined the Court, becoming the second African American justice. In 1981 Sandra Day O'Connor became the first woman justice of the Court.

Although the Supreme Court currently meets in Washington, D.C., its first meeting took place in New York in 1790. The Court maintains certain traditions from its early days, such as justices' wearing of black robes and the placing of white quill pens in the courtroom. Moreover, at each sitting of the Court, the justices shake hands with one another to remind them that, although they may disagree, they share the same purposes.

Reading Time _____

Recalling Facts

1. In 1787 the United States Supreme Court was established by the
   - ❏ a. president.
   - ❏ b. Senate.
   - ❏ c. U.S. Constitution.

2. When the Supreme Court decides cases that have been heard in a lower court, it exercises
   - ❏ a. appellate power.
   - ❏ b. the power to impeach.
   - ❏ c. the power to resolve conflicts between states.

3. In *Brown v. Board of Education of Topeka,* the U.S. Supreme Court ruled that
   - ❏ a. persons who are arrested must be told their rights.
   - ❏ b. having schools separated according to race is contrary to the Constitution.
   - ❏ c. the Supreme Court has the power to decide whether an act of Congress is unconstitutional.

4. The number of justices who serve on the U.S. Supreme Court is
   - ❏ a. six.
   - ❏ b. nine.
   - ❏ c. twelve.

5. The U.S. Supreme Court meets in
   - ❏ a. New York.
   - ❏ b. Washington, D.C.
   - ❏ c. various state capitals.

Understanding Ideas

6. The U.S. Supreme Court
   - ❏ a. is controlled by the president, who appoints members.
   - ❏ b. has jurisdiction over all courts and cases in the United States.
   - ❏ c. has ultimate judicial authority within a narrow range of legal disputes.

7. One can infer that the type of case least likely to be heard by the U.S. Supreme Court is
   - ❏ a. an appeal.
   - ❏ b. a case involving one state against another.
   - ❏ c. a case between two people in court for the first time.

8. If the Supreme Court decided that an act of Congress conflicted with the U.S. Constitution, it would probably
   - ❏ a. negotiate the issue with the Congress.
   - ❏ b. declare the act of Congress unconstitutional.
   - ❏ c. ask the president to veto the act.

9. The person below most likely to be appointed to the Supreme Court is a
   - ❏ a. senator.
   - ❏ b. trial lawyer.
   - ❏ c. lower court judge.

10. One can expect a U.S. Supreme Court justice to
    - ❏ a. make decisions after asking advice from the Senate.
    - ❏ b. make decisions based on knowledge and interpretation of the law and the Constitution.
    - ❏ c. survey the political landscape before making important decisions.

25 B   Oliver Wendell Holmes Jr.: Supreme Court Justice

Oliver Wendell Holmes Jr. was born in Boston, Massachusetts, in 1841. Named for his father, a great writer, Holmes possessed a similar talent for writing. As a young man, he attended Harvard College—writing essays for, and later becoming editor of, the *Harvard Magazine*. Following his graduation, Holmes sustained several injuries on the battlefield for the Union Army in the Civil War. After three years of war service, he returned to Harvard Law School to study law and become an attorney.

Holmes began his career as a lawyer in Boston in 1867. Aside from his duties as an attorney, Holmes lectured on the fundamentals of American law. He also wrote about the subject in a renowned work titled *The Common Law*. After the publication of his book, Holmes taught at Harvard for a term before being appointed to the Massachusetts Supreme Court.

In 1902 Holmes became a justice of the U.S. Supreme Court. Known as the "great dissenter," he often disagreed with the other justices. Holmes frequently wrote his opinions of the law, in defense of such rights as freedom of speech and that of workers to form unions.

Health problems forced Holmes to retire from the Supreme Court in 1932 after serving for 30 years. He died three years later at the age of 93.

1. **Recognizing Words in Context**

   Find the word *dissenter* in the passage. One definition below is closest to the meaning of that word. One definition has the opposite or nearly the opposite meaning. The remaining definition has a completely different meaning. Label the definitions C for *closest*, O for *opposite or nearly opposite*, and D for *different*.

   _____ a. interpreter

   _____ b. supporter

   _____ c. opponent

2. **Distinguishing Fact from Opinion**

   Two of the statements below present *facts*, which can be proved. The other statement is an *opinion*, which expresses someone's thoughts or beliefs. Label the statements F for *fact* and O for *opinion*.

   _____ a. Oliver Wendell Holmes was named for his father, who was a great writer.

   _____ b. Holmes was the wisest person ever to have served on the Supreme Court.

   _____ c. Holmes was known as the "great dissenter."

3. Keeping Events in Order

Number the statements below 1, 2, and 3 to show the order in which the events took place.

_____ a. Holmes began his career as a lawyer in Boston in 1867.

_____ b. Holmes returned to Harvard Law School to study law.

_____ c. Holmes fought for the Union Army in the Civil War.

4. Making Correct Inferences

Two of the statements below are correct *inferences*, or reasonable guesses. They are based on information in the passage. The other statement is an incorrect, or faulty, inference. Label the statements C for *correct* inference and F for *faulty* inference.

_____ a. Holmes pursued a career in law when his writing career failed.

_____ b. Writing was central to Holmes's life.

_____ c. Holmes defended the rights protected by the Constitution.

5. Understanding Main Ideas

One of the statements below expresses the main idea of the passage. One statement is too general, or too broad. The other explains only part of the passage; it is too narrow. Label the statements M for *main idea*, B for *too broad*, and N for *too narrow*.

_____ a. Oliver Wendell Holmes Jr. was a U.S. Supreme Court Justice who served for many years and wrote about the law.

_____ b. The United States has had many illustrious Supreme Court justices.

_____ c. Oliver Wendell Holmes Jr. studied law at Harvard Law School.

Correct Answers, Part A _____

Correct Answers, Part B _____

Total Correct Answers _____

Answer Key

Reading Rate Graph

Comprehension Score Graph

Comprehension Skills Profile Graph

Answer Key

1A	1. b	2. b	3. a	4. a	5. c	6. c	7. c	8. a	9. b	10. b
1B	1. O, C, D	2. F, F, O	3. 2, 1, 3	4. C, F, C	5. B, N, M					
2A	1. b	2. a	3. c	4. b	5. c	6. b	7. a	8. c	9. c	10. c
2B	1. D, O, C	2. O, F, F	3. 3, 1, 2	4. F, C, C	5. N, B, M					
3A	1. c	2. b	3. b	4. b	5. a	6. b	7. b	8. a	9. b	10. b
3B	1. O, D, C	2. F, O, F	3. 3, 2, 1	4. C, C, F	5. B, N, M					
4A	1. b	2. c	3. b	4. c	5. b	6. b	7. a	8. b	9. c	10. b
4B	1. D, O, C	2. F, F, O	3. 1, 3, 2	4. F, C, C	5. N, B, M					
5A	1. b	2. c	3. a	4. c	5. c	6. c	7. b	8. b	9. b	10. c
5B	1. D, C, O	2. F, O, F	3. 3, 1, 2	4. C, F, C	5. B, N, M					
6A	1. c	2. a	3. b	4. c	5. a	6. b	7. a	8. a	9. c	10. b
6B	1. O, C, D	2. O, F, F	3. 2, 3, 1	4. C, C, F	5. B, M, N					
7A	1. a	2. c	3. c	4. a	5. a	6. b	7. b	8. a	9. c	10. b
7B	1. O, C, D	2. F, O, F	3. 2, 1, 3	4. C, F, C	5. N, M, B					
8A	1. c	2. b	3. c	4. c	5. a	6. b	7. b	8. c	9. b	10. b
8B	1. C, O, D	2. F, F, O	3. 1, 2, 3	4. C, C, F	5. M, B, N					
9A	1. b	2. b	3. c	4. c	5. b	6. b	7. a	8. a	9. a	10. b
9B	1. C, D, O	2. O, F, F	3. 2, 1, 3	4. C, F, C	5. B, M, N					
10A	1. a	2. b	3. a	4. c	5. b	6. b	7. c	8. b	9. c	10. c
10B	1. D, C, O	2. F, F, O	3. 3, 1, 2	4. C, C, F	5. N, B, M					
11A	1. a	2. a	3. c	4. a	5. c	6. a	7. c	8. c	9. a	10. b
11B	1. D, O, C	2. F, O, F	3. 1, 3, 2	4. F, C, C	5. B, N, M					
12A	1. c	2. a	3. a	4. a	5. b	6. c	7. b	8. c	9. c	10. a
12B	1. C, O, D	2. F, F, O	3. 2, 1, 3	4. C, F, C	5. N, B, M					
13A	1. a	2. a	3. b	4. c	5. b	6. a	7. a	8. b	9. a	10. c
13B	1. D, C, O	2. O, F, F	3. 1, 3, 2	4. C, C, F	5. M, N, B					

14A	1. c	2. a	3. c	4. c	5. a	6. b	7. a	8. c	9. b	10. c
14B	1. O, D, C		2. F, F, O		3. 3, 2, 1		4. C, F, C		5. N, M, B	
15A	1. c	2. b	3. b	4. c	5. c	6. a	7. b	8. b	9. a	10. a
15B	1. C, O, D		2. F, O, F		3. 2, 1, 3		4. F, C, C		5. M, N, B	
16A	1. a	2. b	3. c	4. b	5. a	6. b	7. a	8. c	9. b	10. c
16B	1. D, O, C		2. F, F, O		3. 2, 3, 1		4. C, C, F		5. N, B, M	
17A	1. c	2. b	3. b	4. c	5. c	6. b	7. a	8. c	9. a	10. b
17B	1. D, C, O		2. O, F, F		3. 3, 2, 1		4. C, F, C		5. N, M, B	
18A	1. c	2. b	3. b	4. c	5. b	6. a	7. c	8. b	9. c	10. c
18B	1. O, D, C		2. F, F, O		3. 1, 2, 3		4. F, C, C		5. B, N, M	
19A	1. c	2. b	3. a	4. b	5. b	6. c	7. b	8. a	9. c	10. b
19B	1. C, O, D		2. F, O, F		3. 2, 1, 3		4. C, C, F		5. N, B, M	
20A	1. b	2. c	3. a	4. a	5. b	6. b	7. c	8. b	9. c	10. a
20B	1. O, C, D		2. F, F, O		3. 3, 2, 1		4. F, C, C		5. N, M, B	
21A	1. a	2. c	3. a	4. c	5. b	6. c	7. a	8. c	9. a	10. c
21B	1. O, D, C		2. O, F, F		3. 3, 1, 2		4. C, F, C		5. M, N, B	
22A	1. b	2. a	3. c	4. c	5. b	6. a	7. b	8. b	9. c	10. b
22B	1. C, D, O		2. F, O, F		3. 2, 3, 1		4. C, C, F		5. M, B, N	
23A	1. a	2. a	3. c	4. c	5. b	6. a	7. c	8. c	9. a	10. a
23B	1. D, C, O		2. O, F, F		3. 3, 2, 1		4. C, F, C		5. B, M, N	
24A	1. b	2. c	3. a	4. a	5. b	6. c	7. c	8. b	9. b	10. b
24B	1. C, O, D		2. F, F, O		3. 3, 1, 2		4. C, C, F		5. M, N, B	
25A	1. c	2. a	3. b	4. b	5. b	6. c	7. c	8. b	9. c	10. b
25B	1. D, O, C		2. F, O, F		3. 3, 2, 1		4. F, C, C		5. M, B, N	

READING RATE

Put an X on the line above each lesson number to show your reading time and words-per-minute rate for that lesson.

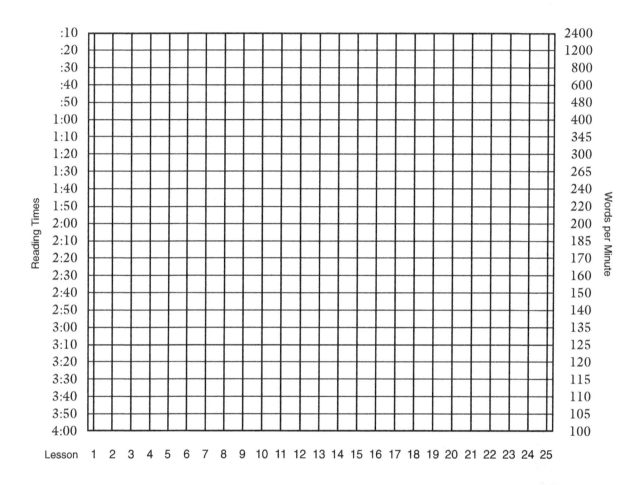

Reading Times		Words per Minute
:10		2400
:20		1200
:30		800
:40		600
:50		480
1:00		400
1:10		345
1:20		300
1:30		265
1:40		240
1:50		220
2:00		200
2:10		185
2:20		170
2:30		160
2:40		150
2:50		140
3:00		135
3:10		125
3:20		120
3:30		115
3:40		110
3:50		105
4:00		100

Lesson 1 2 3 4 5 6 7 8 9 10 11 12 13 14 15 16 17 18 19 20 21 22 23 24 25

COMPREHENSION SCORE

Put an X on the line above each lesson number to indicate your total correct answers and comprehension score for that lesson.

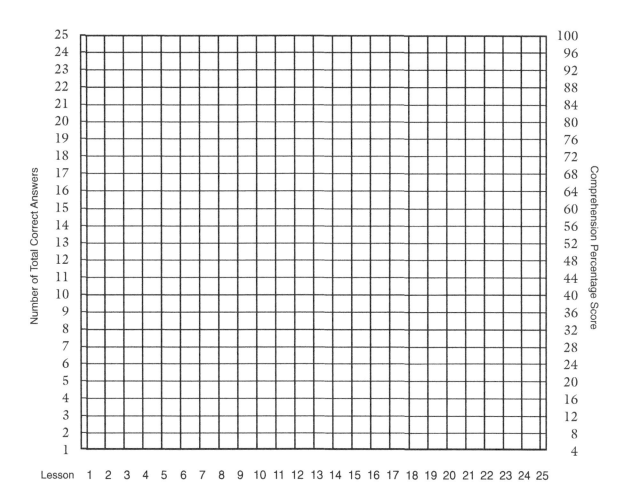

COMPREHENSION SKILLS PROFILE

Put an X in the box above each question type to indicate an incorrect reponse to any part of that question.

	Recognizing Words in Context	Distinguishing Fact from Opinion	Keeping Events in Order	Making Correct Inferences	Understanding Main Ideas
Lesson 1					
2					
3					
4					
5					
6					
7					
8					
9					
10					
11					
12					
13					
14					
15					
16					
17					
18					
19					
20					
21					
22					
23					
24					
25					